Insta

Other Books by the Author

Asian Face Reading: Unlock the Secrets Hidden in the Human Face

Business Guide to Japan: Opening Doors...and Closing Deals

Chinese Etiquette & Ethics in Business

Chinese in Plain English

Discovering Cultural Japan: A Guide to Appreciating and Experiencing the Real Japan

Etiquette Guide to Japan: Know the Rules... that Make the Difference

Instant Japanese

Instant Chinese

Japanese Business Dictionary: English to Japanese

Japanese Etiquette & Ethics in Business

Japanese Influence on America: The Impact, Challenge and Opportunity

Japanese in Plain English

Japan Made Easy—All You Need to Know to Enjoy Japan

Kata: The Key to Understanding and Dealing with the Japanese

Korea's Business and Cultural Code Words

Korean Business Etiquette

Korean in Plain English

Shopper's Guide to Japan

Survival Japanese

The Chinese Have a Word for It: The Complete Guide to Chinese Thought and Culture

The Japanese Have a Word for It: The Complete Guide to Japanese Thought and Culture

Japan's Cultural Code Words: 233 Key Terms That Explain the Attitudes and Behavior of the Japanese

Survival Chinese

Subway Guide to Tokyo: Hundreds of Key Destinations

Instant Korean

How to Express 1,000 Different Ideas
With Just 100 Key Words and Phrases

by Boyé Lafayette De Mente

TUTTLE PUBLISHING
Tokyo • Rutland, Vermont • Singapore

Published by Tuttle Publishing, an imprint of Periplus Editions (HK) Ltd.,
with editorial offices at 364 Innovation Drive, North Clarendon, VT 05759 USA,
and 61 Tai Seng Avenue #02-12 Singapore 534167.

LCC Card No. 2004113424
ISBN 978-0-8048-3596-1

Printed in Singapore

Distributed by:

Japan
Tuttle Publishing
Yaekari Building 3F
5-4-12 Osaki, Shinagawa-ku
Tokyo 141-0032, Japan
Tel: (81) 3 5437 0171   Fax: (81) 3 5437 0755
Email: tuttle-sales@gol.com

North America, Latin America & Europe
Tuttle Publishing
364 Innovation Drive
North Clarendon, VT 05759-9436, USA
Tel: 1 (802) 773 8930   Fax: 1 (802) 773 6993
Email: info@tuttlepublishing.com
www.tuttlepublishing.com

Asia Pacific
Berkeley Books Pte Ltd
61 Tai Seng Avenue #02-12
Singapore 534167
Tel: (65) 6280 1330   Fax: (65) 6280 6290
Email: inquiries@periplus.com.sg
www.periplus.com

14 13 12 11 10   10 9 8 7

CONTENTS

PREFACE

The Korean language has a number of characteristics in common with Chinese and Japanese. These characteristics include their grammatical order (subject, object, verb), the lack of articles (a, an, the), and leaving the subject out of sentences when it is understood from the context.

While these grammatical differences may appear to be an obstacle to English speakers, the trick, when first taking up the study and use of the language, is to ignore the grammatical structure and simply use it the way it is supposed to be used. With this approach, the phrases and sentences you use feel just as "normal" as English.

Some 60 percent of the present-day Korean vocabulary consists of words that were originally Chinese. From around 100 B.C. to 300 A.D. the small kingdoms existing on the Korean peninsula were under the suzerainty of China. During that period, the Koreans adopted the Chinese system of writing, and with it, large numbers of Chinese terms.

In the early 1440s, the king of the unified kingdom of Choson (also spelled Chosun) ordered court scholars to create a new, strictly Korean script for writing both the native Korean and imported Chinese words. This new script, called *Hangul* (Hahn-guhl), was completed in 1446.

But Korea's elite class continued to use the Chinese system of writing up to modern times. Today, the language is still generally written with a combination of Chinese characters and *Hangul*.

Another important factor in the study and use of Korean is that a growing percentage of the daily vocabulary of Koreans is Koreanized English—that is, English words that have been absorbed into the language and are pronounced as if they were Korean.

Camera, for example, is *kamera* (kah-may-rah). Candy is *kaendi* (kahn-dee). Jazz is *jaju* (jah-juu). Jelly is *chelli* (chehl-lee), and so on. In most cases, the Koreanized English words are still recognizable as English.

The English phonetics provided for each Korean word and expression in this book are designed to get as close as possible to the correct pronunciation. As you will see, the pronunciation follows a precise formula which soon becomes familiar. The phonetic versions are hyphenated to make their pronunciation easier. Just pronounce the phonetics as standard English and practice saying them in a smooth, even flow.

The pronunciation of a number of syllables making up the Korean language cannot be reproduced exactly in English phonetics, but since Korean is not tonal (like Chinese) it is generally possible to get close enough to the "correct" pronunciation to be understood.

Koreans are especially tolerant of foreigners who make an effort to speak their language, go out of their way to help them, and do not fault them for speaking with "an accent."

Here are some very important example words to help you get started:

Korea	*Hanguk* (Hahn-guuk) 한국
Korean language	*Hanguk mal* (Hahn-guuk mahl) 한국말
Korean (language)	*Hanguk-o* (Hahn-guuk-aw) 한국어
Korean (person)	*Hanguksaram* (Hahn-guuk-sah-rahm) 한국사람
South Korea	*Nam Han* (Nahm Hahn) 남한
North Korea	*Puk'an* (Puuk-ahn) 북한

The Korean Alphabet, Grammar and Pronunciation Guides

The Korean alphabet consists of 10 vowels and 14 consonants, which are combined to create some 140 syllables, or "building blocks" that make up the language. The building blocks include 11 diphthongs (combinations of vowels and consonants) that are used to represent more complex sounds.

These vowels, consonants, diphthongs and syllables have been rendered into romanized English phonetics by a number of individual scholars as well as by the Cultural Ministry, and there are some differences in them. In 2003, the Korean government issued a new set of rules for transcribing the sounds of the language into Roman letters in an effort to further rationalize the system.

I have made choices from these phonetic versions and added some of my own in an attempt to simplify the pronunciations and still get close enough to the original Korean sounds so that they will be understood.

There are six basic vowels in the Korean alphabet, plus four "y" vowels for a total of ten. Their approximate English sounds are:

A	Ya	O	Yo	O	Yo	U	Yu	U	I
ah	yah	aw	yaw	oh	yoh	uu	yuu	oo	ee

One or more of these 10 basic sounds are used in all of the syllables making up the language.

The diphthongs and their approximate English sounds:

AE	YAE	E	YE	OE	WI	UI	WA	WO	WAE	WE
aa	yay	eh	yeh	oh-eh	wee	we	wah	woh	way	weh

The consonants and their closest English sounds:

k(g) as the **k** in king or the **g** in guy*
n as the **n** in name
t(d) as the **t** in toy or the **d** in day*
r(l) as the **r** in rain or the **l** in lily*
m as the **m** in mother
p(b) as the **p** in pin or the **b** in book*
s as the **s** in speech
ng as the **ng** in king
ch(j) as the **j** in John*
ch' as the **ch** in church
k' as the **k** in kite
t' as the **t** in tank
p' as the **p** in pump
h as the **h** in high

*The "correct" pronunciation of five of these consonants (**k, t, r, p** and **ch**) is very subtle. To the ears of native English speakers, the **k** sound is closer to **g**, the **t** sound is closer to **d**, the **r** is closer to **l**, the **p** is closer to **b** and the **ch** is best represented by the **j** sound.

Koreans who have become fluent in English say there are some sounds in the Korean language that simply cannot be rendered into English phonetics. Fortunately, as with English and other languages, Korean spoken with an "accent" is still understandable.

There are also five "double consonants" (*kk, tt, pp, ss* and *tch*):

kk as the **k** in sky or in jack
tt as the **t** in stay
pp as the **p** in spy

ss   as the *ss* in essential

tch as the *t* in tzar

It is important to stress the pronunciation of consonants at the beginning of words. It is especially important to "hit" the double consonants hard. I have made attempts to account for the double consonants and other features of the language in the phonetics provided for each word and sentence in the book.

Pronunciation Guide for Korean Syllables

To clearly see and hear the repetitions of the 10 vowel sounds in all of the syllables, read the following lines vertically. [About a dozen of these syllables are seldom if ever used.]

A	**YA**	**O**	**YO**	**O**	**YO**	**U**	**YU**	**U**	**I**
ah	yah	aw	yaw	oh	yoh	uu	yuu	oo	ee
GA	**GYA**	**GO**	**GYO**	**GO**	**GYO**	**GU**	**GYU**	**GU**	**GI**
gah	gyah	gaw	gyaw	goh	gyoh	guu	gyuu	goo	ghee
NA	**NYA**	**NO**	**NYO**	**NO**	**NYO**	**NU**	**NYU**	**NU**	**NI**
nah	nyah	naw	nyaw	noh	nyoh	nuu	nyuu	noo	nee
DA	**DYA**	**DO**	**DYO**	**DO**	**DYO**	**DU**	**DYU**	**DU**	**DI**
dah	dyah	daw	dyaw	doh	dyoh	duu	dyuu	doo	dee
LA	**LYA**	**LO**	**LYO**	**LO**	**LYO**	**LU**	**LYU**	**LU**	**LI**
lah	lyah	law	lyaw	loh	lyoh	luu	lyuu	loo	lee
MA	**MYA**	**MO**	**MYO**	**MO**	**MYO**	**MU**	**MYU**	**MU**	**MI**
mah	myah	maw	myaw	moh	myoh	muu	myuu	moo	mee

BA	**BYA**	**BO**	**BYO**	**BO**	**BYO**	**BU**	**BYU**	**BU**	**BI**
bah	byah	baw	byaw	boh	byoh	buu	byuu	byoo	bee

SA	**SYA**	**SO**	**SYO**	**SO**	**SYO**	**SU**	**SYU**	**SU**	**SI**
sah	syah	saw	syaw	soh	syoh	suu	syuu	syoo	she

JA	**JYA**	**JO**	**JYO**	**JO**	**JYO**	**JU**	**JYU**	**JU**	**JI**
jah	jyah	jaw	jyaw	joh	jyoh	juu	jyuu	joo	jee

CHA	**CHYA**	**CHO**	**CHYO**	**CHO**	**CHYO**	**CHU**	**CHYU**	**CHU**	**CHI**
chah	chyah	chuh	chyaw	choh	chyoh	chuu	chyuu	choo	chee

KA	**KYA**	**KO**	**KYO**	**KO**	**KYO**	**KU**	**KYU**	**KU**	**KI**
kah	kyah	kaw	kyaw	koh	kyoh	kuu	kyuu	koo	kee

TA	**TYA**	**TO**	**TYO**	**TO**	**TYO**	**TU**	**TYU**	**TU**	**TI**
tah	tyah	taw	tyaw	toh	tyoh	tuu	tyuu	too	tee

PAH	**PYA**	**PO**	**PYO**	**PO**	**PYO**	**PU**	**PYU**	**PU**	**PI**
pah	pyah	paw	pyaw	poh	pyoh	puu	pyuu	poo	pee

HA	**HYA**	**HO**	**HYO**	**HO**	**HYO**	**HU**	**HYU**	**HU**	**HI**
hah	hyah	haw	hyaw	hoh	hyoh	huu	hyuu	hoo	hee

PART 1

1 Greetings *Insa* (Een-sah) 인사

Hello
Good morning
Good afternoon
Good evening
How are you?
How do you do?

All of these greetings are incorporated in a single Korean expression:
Annyong haseyo (Ahn-n'yohng hah-say-yoh) 안녕하세요

This universal greeting literally means "Are you at peace?" A reply to these greetings, in all cases, may be a repetition of the above phrase preceded by *ne* (naay), which means "yes."

Ne, annyong haseyo
(Naay, ahn-n'nyohng hah-say-yoh) 안녕하세요

More formal versions of these greetings are:
Annyong hashimnikka? (Ahn-n'yohng hah-sheem-nee-kah?) 안녕하십니까?

Ye, annyong hashimnikka (Yay, ahn-n'yohng hah-sheem-nee-kah) 예, 안녕하십니까

Good morning, Mr. Cho.
Cho Sonsaeng Nim, annyong hashimnikka? (Cho Sun-sang Neem, ahn-n'yohng hah-sheem-nee-kah?) 조선생 님, 안녕 하십니까?

Hello, Miss Pak.
Pak Yang, annyong hashimnikka? (Pak Yahng, ahn-n'yohng hah-sheem-nee-kah?) 박양, 안녕하십니까?

Goodnight.
Annyong-hi chumuseyo* (Ahn-yohng-hee chuu-muu-say-yoh) 안녕히 주무세요

*The "*yo*" at the end of so many Korean expressions, including one-word questions or replies, functions as a honorific that makes them polite.

2 # Hello! (To attract someone's attention, and on the telephone)
Yoboseyo! (Yuh-boh-say-yoh!) 여보세요!

3 # Goodbye (A final farewell, said by the person leaving)
Anyong-hi kyeseyo* (Ahn-n'yohng-he kuh-say-yoh) 안녕히 계세요

*The literal meaning of this phrase is "Stay in peace."

Goodbye! (Said by the person not leaving)
Anyong-hi kaseyo (Ahn-yohng-he kah-say-yoh) 안녕히 계세요

Goodbye.
Sugo haseyo (Suu-go hah-say-yoh) 수고하세요

*Said by a person leaving a place of work, literally meaning "work hard."

4 # See you later *Ta nyo o gesseoyo** (Tah n'yoh oh guh-say-yoh) 다녀오겠어요

*Literally, "I will return," said by the person leaving.

See you later.
Ta nyo o seyo* (Tah n'yoh oh say-yoh) 다녀오세요

*Literally, "Please return," said by the person not leaving.

Generic forms:

See you later.
Do poepket ssumnida (Doh pep-keht sume-nee-dah)
또 뵙겠습니다
also:
Do mannap shida (Doh mahn-nahp she-dah) 또 만납시다

5 Please *Chom* (Choam) / *Chebal* (Chuh-bahl) 좀 / 제발

These Korean equivalents of the English word "please,"
chom and *chebal*, are seldom if ever used alone. The concept
of "please" is implied in polite verbs, such as *chushipshio*
(chuu-ship-she-oh), which has the meaning of "please do
…."

One moment, please.
Chamshi kidaryo chushipshio (Chahms-she kee-dah-rio
chuu-ship-she-oh) 잠시 기다려 주십시오

Less formal:

Just a moment, please.
Chamkkan manyo (Chahm-kahn mahn-yoh) 잠깐 만요

Please take me there.
Ka juseyo (Kah juu-say-yoh) 가주세요

Do (it, something) for me, please.
Hae juseyo (Hay juu-say-yoh) 해주세요

6 Thank you *Kamsahamnida* (Kahm-sah-hahm-nee-
dah) 감사합니다
also:

Komapsumnida (Koh-mahp-sume-nee-dah) 고맙습니다

Thank you very much.
Cham komapsumnida (Chahm koh-mahp-suhm-nee-dah)
참 고맙습니다

Thank you very much.
Daedan hi kamsa hamnida (Day-dahn he kahm-sah hahm-nee-dah) 대단히 감사 합니다

You're welcome.
Chon maneyo (Chone mahn-eh-yoh) 천만에요

7 Excuse me.
Mian hamnida (Me-ahn hahm-nee-dah) 미안합니다

I'm sorry.
Choe song hamnida (Cho-eh soong hahm-nee-dah)
죄송합니다

Pardon me.
Josong hamnida (Joh-soong hahm-nee-dah) 죄송합니다

Sorry to disturb you. [When entering an office or home]
Sil lye hamnida (Sheel lay hahm-nee-dah) 실례합니다

8 I *Na (Nah)** 나

*In most ordinary sentences the "I" (*Na*) is left out because it is understood. "He" and "she" are used only rarely because they are also generally understood.

I don't know.
Na-nun morumnida (Nah-nuun moh-rume-nee-dah)
나는 모릅니다

I think so.
Kuroke saenggakamnida (Kuu-roh-kay sang-gahk-ahm-nee-dah) 그렇게 생각합니다

I'm not going.
An ga yo (Ahn-gah-yoh) 안가요

I would like to go.
Ka-go shipsumnida (Kah-go ship-sume-nee-dah)
가고 싶습니다

I want to go to Seoul.
Seoure ka-go shipoyo (Soh-uhl kah-go she-poh-yoh)
서울에 가고 싶어요

I don't understand Korean.
Hangugma-reul chom hae-yo (Hahn-guuk-mah-ruhl
chome hay-yoh) 한국말을 좀 해요

9 We *Uri* (Uh-ree) 우리

Shall we go?
Kal kayo? (Kahl kah-yoh?) 갈까요?

We can't go.
Mot kayo (Maht kah-yoh) 못가요

We're not going.
An gayo (Ahn gah-yoh) 안가요

10 Me *Narul* (nah-ruhl) 나를; *Naege* (Nay-geh) 내게

Let me see it.
Naege poyo chushipshio (Nay-geh poh-yoh chuu-ship-
she-oh) 내게 보여 주십시오

It belongs to me.
Naege sokan koshimnida (Nay-geh soh-kahn kuh-sheem-
nee-dah) 내게 속한 곳 입니다

Please give me a glass of water.
Naege mulhan kop chushipshio (Nay-gay muhl-hahn kope
chuu-ship-she-oh) 내게 물 한 컵 주십시오

11 My *Nae* (Nay) / *Naui* (Nah-we)

Where is my room?
Nae pang odi itchiyo? (Nay pahng ah-dee eet-chee-yoh?)
내 방 어디 있지요?

What is my room number?
Nae pang-un myopon imnikka? (Nay pahng-uun m'yah-pahn eem-nee-kah?) 내 방은 몇 번입니까?

Here is my address.
Igoshi nae chuso imnida (Ee-guh-she nay chuu-soh eem-nee-dah) 이곳이 내 주소입니다

Where is my brief case?
Nae kabang-un odie issumnikka? (Nah kah-bahng-uun ah-dee-eh ees-sume-nee-dah?) 내 가방은 어디에 있습니까?

12 Mine *Naegot* (Nay-gute)

It's mine.
Kugosun naego shimnida (Kuu-guh-suun nay-guh sheem-nee-dah) 그것은 내것입니다

That umbrella is mine.
Ku usanun naegoshimnida (Kuu uu-sah-nuun nay-go-sheem-nee-dah) 그 우산은 내것입니다

13 You *Tangshin* (Tahng-sheen)* 당신

Where do you live?
Eodi saseyo? (Eh-oh-dee sah-say-yoh?) 어디 사세요?

*Keep in mind that the subject (in this case, you) is normally left out when it is understood.

Where are you going?
Odiro ka shimnikka? (Ah-dee-roh kah sheem-nee-kah?)
어디로 가십니까?

What are you doing now?
Chigum mousul hago kye shimnikka? (Chee-guhm mwah-suhl hah-go kay sheem-nee-kah?) 지금 무엇을 하고 계십 니까?

Would you please do me a favor?
Putakaedo chossumnikka? (Puu-tah-kay-doh choh-sume-nee-kah?) 부탁해도 좋습니까?

Are you going?
Kamnika? (Kahm-nee-kah?) 갑니까?

May I take a photo of you?
Saijin chom chigodo doelkkayo? (Sigh-jeen chome chee-guh-doh dwayl-kah-yoh?) 사진 좀 찍어도 될까요?

14 Your(s) *Tangshinui* (Tahng-sheen-we)

Is this yours?
Igosun tanshin-e goshimnika? (Ee-gah-suun than-sheen-eh guh-sheem-nee-kah?) 이것은 당신의 것입니까?

Is this magazine yours?
Igosun tangshin-e chapji imnikka? (Ee-gah-suun tahng-sheen-eh chop-jee eem-nee-kah?) 이것은 당신의 잡지입 니까?

Is that book yours?
Ku chaegun tangshin koshimnikka? (Kuu chay-guun tahng-sheen kuh-sheem-nee-kah?) 그 책은 당신 것입니 까?

15 He / She / Him / Her *Kunun* (kuu-nuun)

Who is he?
Kunun nugu shimnikka? (Kuu-nuun nuu-guu sheem-nee-kah?) 그는 누구십니까?

She

Kuyojanun (kuu-yoe-jah-nuun) 그여자는

She (he) is not here.

Yogi an kushimnida (Yuh-ghee ahn kuu-sheem-nee-dah)
여기 안계십니다

He *Kuege* (kway-gay) 그에게; *kurul* (kuu-ruhl) 그를

Please give him the money.

Kuege ton-ul chushio (Kway-gay tone-uhl chuu-she-oh)
그에게 돈을 주시요

Her *Kunyoe-ge* (kuun-yway-guh) 그녀에게
also:
kunnyo-rul (kuun-n'yoe-ruhl) 그녀를

Please give her the book.

Kunyoege ku chaegul chushio (Kuun-yway-guh kuu chay-guhl chuu-she-oh) 그녀에게 그 책을 주시오

Please give this to her.

Igosul kuyojae-ge chushipshio (Ee-guh-suhl kuu-yoh-jay-guh chuu-ship-she-oh) 이것을 그녀에게 주십시오

16 Names *Irum* (ee-rume) 이름

What is your name?

Irum-i mwo shimnikka? (Ee-rume-ee mwah sheem-nee-kah?) 이름이 무엇입니까?

I am (my name is) Boyé.

Na-nun Boyé imnida (Nah-nuun Boh-yeh eem-nee-dah)
나는 보예입니다

What is her name?

Kuyoja-ui irumi mwoshimnikka? (Kuu-yoh-jah-we ee-ruum-ee mwah-sheem-nee-kah?) 그 여자의 이름이 무엇입니까?

Please write down your name and address.
Tangshin-e irumgwa chusorul so chushipshio (Tahng-sheen-eh ee-ruum-gwah chuu-suh-ruhl suh chuu-ship-she-oh) 당신의 이름과 주소를 써주십시오

17 Family Names *Song* (Sahng) 성

What is your family name?
Tangshinui songun muo shimnikka? (Tahng-sheen-we suung-guun mwah sheem-nee-kah?) 당신의 성은 무엇입니까?

My family name is De Mente.
Na-ui song De Mente imnida (Nah-we sahng De Mente eem-nee-dah) 나의 성은 데 멘테입니다

How do you spell your family name?
Tangsin-e songul ottoke ssumnikka? (Tahng-sheen-ee sahng-ule ah-tah-keh sume-nee-kah?) 당신의 성을 어떻게 씁니까?

Please write it down.
Ssuseyo (Suu-say-yoh) 쓰세요

18 Name-Card *Myong-ham* (M'yohng-hahm) 명함

Here's my name-card.
Che myong-ham ie yo (Chuh m'yohng-ham ee-eh yoh) 제 명함이에요

May I have your card?
Myong-ham han chang chushigesseoyo? (M'yohng-ham hahn chahng chuu-she-geh-say-oh-yoh?) 명함 한 장 주시겠어요?

I'm pleased to meet you. (Literally, "I'm seeing you for the first time.")
Choum poepkessumnida (Choh-uhm pep-kay-sume-nee-dah) 처음 뵙겠습니다

19 **Age** *Yonse* (Yuhn-seh) 연세; *Nai* (Nigh) 나이

How old are you?
Yonse-ga myochi ishimnikka? (Yuhn-seh-gah m'yoe-chee
ee-sheem-nee-kah?) 연세가 몇이십니까?
also:
Nai-ga olma imnikka? (Nigh-gah ohl-mah eem-nee-kah?)
나이가 얼마입니까?

I am _____ years old.
Chonun _____ sarieo (Choh-nuun _____ sah-ree-eh-
oh) 저는 _____ 살이예요

How old is your daughter / son?
Dal-e / adul-e naiga ottoke dwaeyo? (Dahl-eh / ah-duhl-eh
nigh-gah aht-tuh-kuh dway-yoh?) 딸의 / 아들의 나이가
어떻게 돼요?

20 **Family** *Kajong* (Kah-juung) 가정; *Kajok* (Kah-joak)
가족

father	*aboji* (ah-boh-jee) 아버지
grandfather	*haraboji* (hah-rah-boh-jee) 할아 버지
dad	*appa* (ahp-pah) 아빠
mother	*omoni* (oh-moh-nee) 어머니
grandmother	*halmoni* (hahl-moh-nee) 할머니
your husband	*nampyon* (nahm-p'yohn) 남편
my husband	*chuin* (chuu-een) 주인
my wife	*anae* (ah-nay) 아내
his/your wife	*puin* (puu-een) 부인
parents	*yangchin* (yahng-cheen) 양친; *pumo* (puu-moh) 부모
granddaughter	*sonnyo* (soan-n'yuh) 손녀
grandson	*sonja* (soan-jah) 손자

This is my husband.

Ibunun uri nampyonieyo (Ee-buu-nuun uu-ree nahm-p'yohn ee-eh-yoh)) 이분은 우리 남편이에요.

This is my wife.

Ibunun uri annae eyo (Ih-buu-nuun uu-ree ahn-nay eh-yoh) 이분은 우리 아내에요.

Are your parents still living?

Yangchain kkesonun saengjonhae kyeshimnikka? (Yahng-chah-een kuh-suhn-uhn sang-jon-hay kay-sheem-nee-kah?) 양친 께서는 생존해 계십니까?

21 Children *Chanyoga* (Chahn-yuh-gah)

daughter	*dal* (dahl) 딸
son	*adul* (ah-duhl) 아들
grandchildren	*sonju* (soan-juu) 손주

How many children do you have?

Chanyo-ga myon-myong iseyo? (Chah-yuh-gah m'yuhn-m'yuhng ee-seh-yoh?) 자녀가 몇 명이세요?

I have two daughters.

Na egenun dal hana-ga issumnida (Nah eh-geh-nuhn dahl hah-nah-gah ee-sume-nee-dah) 나에게는 딸 하나가 있습니다

Do you have grandchildren?

Sonju issu seyo? (Sohn-juu ee-suh-say-yoh?) 손주 있으세요?

22 Who? *Nugu* (Nuu-guu) 누구

Who are you?

Taegun nugu shimnikka? (Tay-guun nuu-guu sheem nee-kah?) 댁은 누구 십니까?

Who is that?

Kuge nugujiyo? (Kuu-gay nuu-guu-jee-yoh?) 그게 누구
지요?

Who is that man?

Chobunun nugu shimnikka? (Choh-buu-nuun nuu-guu
sheem-nee-kah?) 저분은 누구십니까?

23 What? *Muot* (Mwaht) 무엇

What is this?

Igosun muoshijiyo? (Ee-guh-suun mwah-she-jee-yoh?) 이
것은 무엇이지요?

What is the price?

Kapshi olma jiyo? (Kop-she ohl-mah jee-yoh?) 값이 얼
마지요?

What did you say?

Muorago hasyotchiyo? (Mwah-rah-go hah-shoat-chee-
yoh?) 워라고 하셨지요?

What does _____ mean?

_____ *ga musun dushieyo?* (_____ gah muu-suhn duu-
she eh-yoh?) ____ 가 무슨 뜻이에요?

What are you doing?

Mwo haseyo? (Mwoh hah-say-yoh?) 뭐 하세요?

What is this called in Korean?

Hangung-mal lo meorago haeyo? (Hahn-guug-mahl loh
mwah-rah-go hay-yoh?) 한국말로 뭐라고 해요?

24 When? *Onje* (Ahn-jeh) 언제?

When? *Onje?* (Ahn-jeh?) 언제?

When shall we start?
Onje ttonalkkayo? (Ahn-jeh tohn-ahl-kah-yoh?) 언제 떠
날까요?

When will it end (be over)?
Todaeche onje kunnajiyo? (Toh-day-chee ahn-juh kuhn-
nah-jee-yoh?) 도대체 언제 끝나지요?

25 Where? (in/to what place) *Odiro* (Ah-dee-ruh) 어디로

Where are you going?
Odiro kashim nikka? (Ah-dee-ruh kah-sheem nee-kah?)
어디로 가십니까?

26 Where? (at what place) *Odiso* (Ah-dee-suh) 어디서

Where do you live?
Odiso salgo kyeshim nikka? (Ah-dee-suh sahl-go kay-
sheem nee-kah?) 어디서 살고 계십니까?

Where is the station?
Yok odiso issumnikka? (Yuhk ah-dee-suh ees-sume-nee-
kah?) 역이 어디 있습니까?

Where can I buy a guidebook on Seoul?
Seoul kwangwang annae so-rul odiso sal su issoyo?
(Seoul kwahn-gwahng ahn-nay suh-ruhl ah-dee-suh sahl
suu ee-suh-yoh?) 서울 관광 안내서를 어디서 살 수
있어요?

27 Why? *Wae* (way) 왜? / *Wae-yo* (Way-yoh) 왜요?

Why not?
Wae an toejiyo? (Way ahn tway-joe?) 왜 안 되지요?

28 **How?** *Ottoke* (Aht-tah-keh) 어떻게

How are you doing?

Ottoke chinae shimnikka? (Aht-tah-kay chee-nay sheem-nee-kah?) 어떻게 지내십니까?

How old are you?

Myot sarim nikka? (M'yaht sah-reem nee-kah?) 몇 살입니까?

How many are there?

Olmana mani issumnikka? (Ohl-mah-nah mah-nee ee-sume-nee-kah?) 얼마나 많이 있습니까?

How much do you want?

Olmana piryo hamnikka? (Ohl-mah-nah pee-rio hahm-nee-kah?) 얼마나 필요합니까?

How do you say _____?

_____ *rul mworago haeyo?* (_____ ruhl mwah-rah-go hay-yoh?) _____ 를 뭐라고 해요?

29 **This** *Igot* (Ee-gut) 이것

What is this?

Igotsun muoshimnikka? (Ee-gut-suun mwah-sheem-nee-kah?) 이것은 무엇입니까?

Is this yours?

Igotsun tangshin-e gushimnika? (Ee-gut-suun tahng-sheen-eh guh-sheem-nee-kah?) 이것은 당신의 것입니까?

This belongs to me.

Igutsun nagu shimnida (I-gut-suun nah-guu sheem-nee-dah) 이것은 내 것 입니다.

30 **That** *Ku* (Kuh) 그; *Kugot* (Kuh-gut) 그것

What is that?
Kugosun muoshijiyo? (Kuu-guh-suun mwah-she-jee-yoh?) 그것은 무엇이지요?

Who is that?
Ku-ge nuguijiyo? (Kuu-geh nuu-gwee-jee-yoh?) 그게 누구지요?

Who is calling (on the phone)?
Nugu shimnikka? (Nuu-guu sheem-nee-kah?) 누구 십니까?

31 **Which?** *Onu* (Ah-nuh) 어느

Which do you like better, tea or coffee?
Cha wa kopi chung onu tchogul choahashim nikka?
(Chah wah koh-pee chuung ah-nuh choe-guhl choh-ah-hah-sheem nee-kah?) 차와 커피 중 어느 것을 좋아하십니까?

Which one of you will go with me?
Nuga nahago kachi karyomnikka? (Nuu-gah nah-hah-go kah-chee kah-r'yuhm-nee-kah?) 누가 나하고 같이 가렵니까?

32 **Yes / No** * *Ye* (Yeh) 예; *Ne* (Neh) 네 / *Anio* (Ah'nyoh) 아니오

"Yes" and "No" are used in Korean very much like they are in English, separately and at the beginning of responses.

Yes, that's right.
Ne, majayo (Nay, mah-jah-yoh) 네, 맞아요.

No, that's not right

Anio, an guraeyo (Ah-n'yoh ahn guh-ray-yoh) 아니오, 안 그래요

33 Go *Ka* (kah) (Sometimes pronounced as gah) 가

I am going.

Ka yo (Kah yoh) 가요

I am not going.

An gayo (Ahn gah-yoh) 안 가요
or:
Kaji anayo (Kah-jee ah-nah-yoh) 가지 않아요.

I can go tomorrow.

Chonun naeil kalsu issoyo (Choh-nuun nay-eel kahl-suu ee-suh-yoh) 저는 내일 갈 수 있어요.

I can't go.

Mot ka yo (Maht kah yoh) 못가요.

Let's go.

Kap shida (Kahp she-dah) 갑시다.

Let's go for a walk.

San chaekaro kapshida (Sahn chake-ah-roh kahp-she-dah) 산책하러 갑시다.

Where are you going?

Odi kaseyo? (Ah-dee kah-say-yoh?) 어디 가세요?

34 Speak *Marul* (Mah-ruhl) 말을 / *Ihae* (Ee-hay) 이해

I speak a little Korean.

Hangung-mal-rul chom hae yo (Hahn-guug-mahl-ruhl choam hay-yoh) 한국말을 좀 해요.

Please speak slowly.

Chon-chon-hi mal soum-haseyo (Chohn-chohn-he mahl so-uum hah-say-yoh) 천천히 말씀 하세요.

Please repeat that.
Tashi hanbon malhae juseyo (Tah-shee hahn-bun mahl-hay juu-say-yoh) 다시 한 번 말해 주세요.

May I speak with you?
Iyagi kachi nanuodo chokessumnikka? (Ee-yah-ghee kah-chee nah-nway-doh choak-eh-sume-nee-kah?) 이야기 같이 나눠도 좋겠습니까?

35 Understand *Ihae* (Ee-hay) 이해; *Alda* (Ahl-dah) 알 다.

Do you understand?
Ara durushossoyo? (Ah-rah duh-ruh-shuh-suh-yoh?) 알아 들으셨어요?

Yes, I understand.
Ye, al-ge sseo yo (Yeh, ahl-guh soh yoh) 예, 알겠어요.

I don't understand.
Moruget ssumnida (Moh-ruu-geht sume-nee-dah) 모르겠 습니다.

Please write it down.
I chongie-sseo chuseyo (Ee chohng-ee-eh say-oh chuu-say-yoh) 이 종이에 써주세요.

What is this called in Korean?
Hangun mal-lo meorago haeyo? (Hahn-guun mahl-loh mwoh-rah-go hay-yoh?) 한국 말로 뭐라고 해요?

36 English *Yong-O* (Yuhng-Ah) 영어

Do you speak English?
Yong-O haseyo? (Yuhng-Ah hah-say-yoh?) 영어 하세요?

Do you speak English?
Yong-O-rul hashimnikka? (Yuhng-Uh-ruhl hah-sheem-nee-kah?) 영어를 하십니까?

Does anyone speak English?

Yong-O hashinunbun kyeseo? (Yuhng-Ah hah-she-nuhn-boon kay-say-yoh?) 영어 하시는분 계세요?

37 The Numbers* *Sutcha* (Suut-chah) 숫자

Two sets of numbers are used in Korea. One is based on the native Korean system, and the other is derived from the Chinese system. The Korean system goes up to only 99. From 100 on, only the Chinese system is used.

Generally, the Korean set of numbers is used when counting things in smaller units, like the hours from 1 through 12. However, all minutes are counted with the Chinese set of numerals. The names of the months also use Chinese numerals (1st month = January, 2nd month = February, etc.).

The Cardinal Numbers [Chinese]

0	*kong* (kong) 공 / *yong* (yuhng) 영	
1	*il* (eel) 일	
2	*i* (ee) 이	
3	*sam* (sahm) 삼	
4	*sa* (sah) 사	
5	*o* (oh) 오	
6	*yuk* (yuke) 육	
7	*chil* (cheel) 칠	
8	*p'al* (pahl) 팔	
9	*ku* (kuu) 구	
10	*sip* (ship) 십	
11	*sibil* (she-beel) 십일	
12	*sibi* (she-bee) 십이	
13	*sipsam* (ship-sahm) 십삼	
14	*sipsa* (ship-sah) 십사	
15	*sibo* (she-boh) 십오	
16	*sipyuk* (ship-yuhk) 십육	
17	*sipchil* (ship-cheel) 십칠	
18	*sippal* (ship-pahl) 십팔	

19	*sipgu* (ship-guu) 십구
20	*osip* (ee-ship) 이십
21	*isibil* (ee-she-beel) 이십일
22	*isibi* (ee-she-bee) 이십이
23	*isipsam* (ee-ship-sam) 이십삼
24	*isipsa* (ee-ship-sah) 이십사
25	*isipo* (ee-she-boh) 이십오
26	*isipyuk* (ee-ship-yuhk) 이십육
27	*isipch'il* (ee-ship-cheel) 이십칠
28	*isipp'al* (ee-ship-pahl) 이십팔
29	*isipgu* (ee-ship-guu) 이십구
30	*samsip* (sahm-ship) 삼십
40	*sasip* (sah-ship) 사십
50	*osip* (oh-ship) 오십
60	*yuksip* (yuhk-ship) 육십
70	*ch'ilsip* (cheel-ship) 칠십
80	*palsip* (pahl-ship) 팔십
90	*kusip* (kuu-ship) 구십
100	*baek* (bake) 백
101	*baekil* (bake-eel) 백일
102	*baeki* (bake-ee) 백이
200	*ibaek* (ee-bake) 이백
300	*sambaek* (sahm-bake) 삼백
400	*sabaek* (sah-bake) 사백
1,000	*chon* (chahn) 천
10,000	*man* (mahn) 만
20,000	*iman* (ee-mahn) 이만
30,000	*samman* (sahm-mahn) 삼만
40,000	*saman* (sah-mahn) 사만
50,000	*oman* (oh-mahn) 오만
100,000	*shimman* (sheem-mahn) 십만
200,000	*ishimman* (ee-sheem-mahn) 이십만
1 million	*paeng man* (pang-mahn) 백만

Cardinal Numbers [Native Korean]

1	*hana* (hah-nah)	하나
2	*tul* (tuhl)	둘
3	*set* (sate)	셋
4	*net* (nate)	넷
5	*tasot* (tah-sut)	다섯
6	*yosot* (yuh-sut)	여섯
7	*ilgop* (eel-gope)	일곱
8	*yodol* (yuh-duhl)	여덟
9	*ahop* (ah-hap)	아홉
10	*yol* (yuhl)	열
11	*yol-hana* (yuhl-hah-nah)	열하나
12	*yoldul* (yuhl-duhl)	열둘
13	*yol-set* (yuhl-sate)	열셋
14	*yol-net* (yuhl-nate)	열넷
15	*yoldasot* (yuhl-dah-sut)	열다섯
16	*yolyosot* (yuhl-yuh-sut)	열여섯
17	*yorilgop* (yuhl-reel-gupe)	열일곱
18	*yoryodol* (yuhl-ryuh-duhl)	열여덟
19	*yorahop* (yuh-rah-hope)	열아홉
20	*somul* (suh-muhl)	스물
30	*sorun* (suh-ruhn)	서른
40	*mahun* (mah-huhn)	마흔
50	*shwin* (sh-ween)	쉰
60	*yesun* (yeh-suun)	예순
70	*irun* (ee-ruhn)	이른
80	*yodun* (yuu-duhn)	여든
90	*ahun* (ah-huhn)	아흔

Ordinal Numbers [Native Korean]

1st	*ch'ot-jjae* (choat-jay)	첫째
2nd	*tul-jjae* (tuhl-jay)	둘째
3rd	*se-jjae* (say-jay)	세째
4th	*ne-jjae* (nay-jay)	네째
5th	*tasot-jjae* (tah-sut-jay)	다섯째

6th	*yosot-jjae* (yaw-sut-jay)	여섯째
7th	*ilgop-jjae* (eel-gupe-jay)	일곱째
8th	*yodol-jjae* (yah-duhl-jay)	여덟째
9th	*ohop-jjae* (oh-hap-jay)	아홉째
10th	*yol-jjae* (yuhl-jay)	열째

38 Counting *Kyesan* (Kay-sahn)

Like Chinese and Japanese, Korean makes use of special "classifiers" or "markers" when counting people and things. The common classifier for people is *saram* (sah-rahm). [An honorific term, *pun* (poon), is used when the occasion calls for it.] When counting people and things up to 100, native Korean numerals may be used. For everything above 100, numerals derived from Chinese are used.

one person	*han saram* (hahn sah-rahm)	한 사람
two persons	*tul saram* (tuhl sah-rahm)	두 사람
three persons	*set saram* (sate sah-rahm)	세 사람
four persons	*net saram* (nate sah-rahm)	네 사람
five persons	*tasot saram* (tah-sut sah-rahm) 다섯 사람	

There are well over a dozen classifiers for different kinds and categories of things. But there is also a "universal classifier"—*kae* (kay)—that may be used when one is in doubt about the "correct" one. The classifiers come after the appropriate number.

universal classifier:	*kae* (kay) 개
animals and fish:	*mari* (mah-ree) 마리
books, magazines, notebooks:	*kwon* (kwahn) 권
bottles (of beer, water, etc.):	*byong* (b'yung) 병
boxes and packages:	*kap* (kahp) 갑
buildings and houses:	*chae* (chay) 채
building floors:	*chung* (chuung) 층
cars and other machines:	*tae* (tay) 대

paper, bills, tickets, etc.:   *jang* (jahng) 장
slender things like pencils,
sticks: *charu* (chah-ruu) 자루

Two sheets of paper, please.
Tu jang juseyo (Tuu jahng juu-say-yoh) 두 장 주세요

Three tickets, please.
Pyo se jang juseyo (P'yoh seh jahng juu-say-yoh)
표 세 장 주세요.

Two glasses of beer, please.
Maekchu tu jan juseyo (Make-juu tuu jahn juu-say-yoh)
맥주 두 잔 주세요.

Two bottles of beer, please.
Maekchu tu byong, juseyo (Make-juu tuu b'yung, juu-say-yoh) 맥주 두 병 주세요.

39 Time

(In the sense of hours) *Shigan* (She-gahn) 시간
(As in period of time) *Kigan* (Lee-gahn) 기간

minute	*pun* (poon) 분 or *bun* (boon) 분	
hour	*shigan* (she-gahn) 시간	
o'clock	*shi* (she) 시	
a.m.	*ojon* (oh-jahn) 오전	
p.m.	*ohu* (oh-huu) 오후	

A combination of Korean and Chinese numbers are used in telling time. The hours are expressed in native Korean numbers, some of which are abbreviated. Minutes are expressed in numbers derived from Chinese.

1 o'clock	*han shi* (hahn she) 한 시	
2 o'clock	*tu shi* (tuu she) 두 시	
3 o'clock	*se shi* (say she) 세 시	

4 o'clock	*ne shi* (nay she) 네 시
5 o'clock	*tasot shi* (tah-sut she) 다섯 시
6 o'clock	*yosot shi* (yuu-sut she) 여섯 시
7 o'clock	*ilgop shi* (eel-gupe she) 일곱 시
8 o'clock	*yodol shi* (yoh-dahl she) 여덟 시
9 o'clock	*ahop shi* (ah-hope she) 아홉 시
10 o'clock	*yol shi* (yohl she) 열 시
11 o'clock	*yolhan shi* (yohl-hahn she) 열한 시
12 o'clock	*yolttu shi* (yohl-duu she) 열두 시

Minutes are expressed using adapted Chinese numbers:

1 minute	*il bun* (eel boon) 일 분
2 minutes	*i bun* (ee boon) 이 분
3 minutes	*sam bun* (sahm boon) 삼 분
4 minutes	*sa bun* (sah boon) 사 분
5 minutes	*o bun* (oh boon) 오 분
6 minutes	*yuk ppun* (yuhk poon) 육 분
7 minutes	*ch'il bun* (cheel boon) 칠 분
8 minutes	*p'al bun* (pahl boon) 팔 분
9 minutes	*ku bun* (kuu boon) 구 분
10 minutes	*ship ppun* (ship poon) 십 분
11 minutes	*ship-il bun* (ship-eel boon) 십일 분
12 minutes	*ship-i bun* (ship-ee boon) 십이 분
13 minutes	*ship-sam bun* (ship-sahm boon) 십삼 분
14 minutes	*ship-sa bun* (ship-sah boon) 십사 분
15 minutes	*ship-o bun* (ship-oh boon) 십오 분
16 minutes	*shim-nyuk ppun* (sheem-n'yuhk poon) 십육 분
17 minutes	*ship-ch'il bun* (ship-cheel boon) 십칠 분
18 minutes	*ship-p'al bun* (ship-pahl boon) 십팔 분
19 minutes	*ship-kku bun* (ship-kuu boon) 십구 분
20 minutes	*i-ship ppun* (ee-ship poon) 이십 분
21 minutes	*i-ship-il bun* (ee-ship-eel boon) 이십일 분
22 minutes	*i-ship-i bun* (ee-ship-ee boon) 이십이 분

23 minutes	*i-ship-sam bun* (ee-ship-sahm boon) 이십삼 분
24 minutes	*i-ship-sa bun* (ee-ship-sah boon) 이십사 분
25 minutes	*i-ship-o bun* (ee-ship-oh boon) 이십오 분
26 minutes	*i-shim-nyuk ppun* (ee-sheem-n'yuhk poon) 이십육 분
27 minutes	*i-ship-ch'il bun* (ee-ship-cheel boon) 이십칠 분
28 minutes	*i-ship-p'al bun* (ee-ship-pahl boon) 이십팔 분
29 minutes	*i-ship-kku bun* (ee-ship-kuu boon) 이십구 분
30 minutes	*sam-ship ppun* (sahm-ship poon) 삼십 분
40 minutes	*sa-ship ppun* (sah-ship poon) 사십 분
50 minutes	*o-ship ppun* (oh-ship poon) 오십 분
51 minutes	*o-ship-il bun* (oh-ship-eel boon) 오십일 분
52 minutes	*o-ship-i bun* (oh-ship-ee boon) 오십이 분
53 minutes	*o-ship-sam bun* (oh-ship-sahm boon) 오십삼 분
54 minutes	*o-ship-sa bun* (oh-ship-sah boon) 오십사 분
55 minutes	*o-ship-o bun* (oh-ship-oh boon) 오십오 분

What time is it?

Myot shi imnikka? (M'yaht she eem-nee-kkah?)
몇 시입니까?

It's 4 o'clock.

Ne shi yeyo (Nay she yay-yoh) 네시예요.

It's 4:30.

Ne shi pan (Nay she pahn) 네 시 반

Five minutes after four.

Ne shi obun. (Nay she oh-boon) 네 시 오 분

Fifteen minutes after five.
Tasot shi shibo bun (Tah-saht she she-boh boon)
다섯시 십오분

Designations for a.m. and p.m. are placed before the hour, as in:

It is 12 p.m.
Ohu yoltu shi imnida (Oh-huu yahl-tuu she eem-nee-dah)
오후 열두시 입니다.

It's 6:30 p.m.
Ohu yasot shi samship pun. (Oh-huu yah-saht she sahm-ship poon) 오후 여섯시 삼십분

It's 6:30 a.m.
Ojon yasot shi samship pun (Oh-joan yah-saht she sahm-ship poon) 오전 여섯시 삼십분

night	*pam* (pahm) 밤; *yagan* (yah-gahn) 야간
at night	*pame* (pah-may) 밤에
all night/overnight	*pamsaedorok* (pahm-say-doh-roak) 밤새도록
every night	*pammada* (pahm-mah-dah) 밤마다
tonight	*onul chonyok* (oh-nuhl chun-yuk) 오늘 저녁
last night	*kanbam* (kahn-bahm) 간밤
tomorrow	*naeil* (nay-eel) 내일
See you tomorrow	*Naeil poepkessumnida* (Nay-eel pope-keh-sume-nee-dah) 내일 뵙겠습니다
tomorrow morning	*naeil achim* (nay-eel ah-cheem) 내일 아침
tomorrow evening	*naeil chonyok* (nay-eel chun-yuhk) 내일 저녁

40 Days *Yoil* (Yoe-eel)

Sunday	*Ilyoil* (Eel-yoe-eel) 일요일
Monday	*Wolyoil* (Wuhl-yoe-eel) 월요일
Tuesday	*Hwayoil* (Whah-yoe-eel) 화요일
Wednesday	*Suyoil* (Suu-yoe-eel) 수요일
Thursday	*Mokyoil* (Moke-yoe-eel) 목요일
Friday	*Kumyoil* (Kuhm-yoe-eel) 금요일
Saturday	*Toyoil* (Toe-yoe-eel) 토요일
today	*onul* (oh-nuhl) 오늘
tomorrow	*naeil* (nay-eel) 내일
day after tomorrow	*mo-re* (moh-reh) 모레
day before yesterday	*ku jo ke* (kuu joh keh) 그저께
early morning	*sae byok* (say b'yuk) 새벽
afternoon	*ohu* (oh-huu) 오후

What day is today?
Onu-run musun yoil-i-e yo? (Oh-nuu-ruun muu-suun yohl ee-eh yoh?) 오늘은 무슨 요일이에요?

41 Counting Days

Days, in smaller numbers, are generally counted using the native Korean set of numerals, with the terms abbreviated.

one day	*haru* (hah-ruu) 하루
two days	*i teul* (ee tulh) 이틀
three days	*sa heul* (sah huhl) 사흘
four days	*na heul* (nah huhl) 나흘
five days	*tat sae* (taht say) 닷새
six days	*yot sae* (yaht say) 엿새
seven days	*i re* (ee ray) 이레
eight days	*yodu re* (yah-duh ray) 여드레
nine days	*ahu re* (ah-huu ray) 아흐레
ten days	*yo reul* (yah ruhl) 열흘

42 Weeks *Chu* (Chuu) 주

a week's time	*chugan* (chuu-gahn)	주간
this week	*ibon chu* (ee-bohn chuu)	이번 주
last week	*chinan ju* (chee-nahn juu)	지난 주
next week	*taum chu* (tah-uum chuu)	다음 주
every week	*mae ju* (may juu)	매 주
weekday	*pyongil* (p'yohng-eel)	평일
weekend	*chumal* (chuu-mahl)	주말

43 Counting Weeks

Weeks are normally counted using the Chinese set of numbers.

one week	*il chuil* (eel juu-eel)	일주일
two weeks	*i chuil* (ee juu-eel)	이주일
three weeks	*sam chuil* (sahm juu-eel)	삼주일
four weeks	*sa chuil* (sah juu-eel)	사주일
five weeks	*o chuil* (oh juu-eel)	오주일
six weeks	*yuk chuil* (yuuk juu-eel)	육주일
seven weeks	*chil juil* (cheel juu-eel)	칠주일
eight weeks	*pal juil* (pahl juu-eel)	팔주일
nine weeks	*ku chuil* (kuu juu-eel)	구주일
ten weeks	*ship chuil* (ship juu-eel)	십주일

44 Months *Wol* (Wahl)

The terms for the months are combinations of the Chinese numbers 1 through 12, plus *wol* (wahl) for "month". *Tal* (tahl) is another word for "month".

January	*Irwol* (Eer-wuhl)	일월
February	*Iwol* (Ee-wuhl)	이월
March	*Samwol* (Sahm-wuhl)	삼월
April	*Sawol* (Sah-wuhl)	사월

May	*Owol* (Oh-wuhl) 오월	
June	*Yuwol* (Yuu-wuhl) 유월	
July	*Chilwol* (Cheel-wuhl) 칠월	
August	*Palwol* (Pahl-wuhl) 팔월	
September	*Kuwol* (Kuu-wuhl) 구월	
October	*Shiwol* (She-wuhl) 시월	
November	*Shibilwol* (She-beel-wuhl) 십일월	
December	*Shibiwol* (She-bee-wuhl) 십이월	
this month	*i dal* (ee dahl) 이달	
last month	*chinan dal* (chee-nahn dahl) 지난달	
next month	*taum tal* (tah-uum dahl) 다음달	
one month	*han tal* (hahn dahl) 한달	

45 Years *Hae* (Hay) 해

Nyon (N'yuhn) – when in compounds

this year	*kum nyon* (kuum n'yuhn) 금년
next year	*nae nyon* (nay n'yuhn) 내년
last year	*chang nyon* (chahng n'yuhn) 작년
every year	*mae nyon* (may n'yuhn) 매년
New Year's Day	*Sol Lal* (Sohl Lahl) 설날

I wish you a Happy NewYear!
Saehae pok mani padushipshio!
(Say-ahy poak mah-nee pah-duh-ship-she-oh) 새해 복
많이 받으세요.

46 Counting Years

Years are normally counted with the Chinese set of numerals.

one year	*il nyon* (eel n'yun) 일년
two years	*i nyon* (ee n'yun) 이년
three years	*sam nyon* (sahm n'yun) 삼년
four years	*sa nyon* (sah n'yun) 사년
five years	*o nyon* (oh n'yun) 오년

six years	*yung nyon* (young n'yun)	육년
seven years	*chil nyon* (cheel n'yun)	칠년
eight years	*pal nyon* (pahl n'yun)	팔년
nine years	*ku nyon* (kuu n'yun)	구년
ten years	*shim nyon* (sheem n'yun)	십년

47 Money

Money	*Ton* (Tone) 돈;
	Kumjon (Kuum-john) 금전

Korean currency *won* (won/wan). *Won* coins come in six denominations:

1 won	*il won* (eel won)	일원
5 won	*o won* (oh won)	오원
10 won	*ship won* (sheep won)	십원
50 won	*oship won* (oh-sheep won)	오십원
100 won	*paek won* (bake won)	백원
500 won	*o-baek won* (oh-bake won)	오백원

Notes or bills come in three denominations:

1,000 won	*chon won* (chone won)	천원
5,000 won	*ochon won* (oh-chone won)	오천원
10,000 won	*man won* (mahn won)	만원

money changer	*hwan gumsang* (wahn guum-sahng) 환금상
exchange rate	*hwanyul* (hwahn-yuhl) 환율
U.S. dollars	*dallo* (dahl-lah) 달러
Japanese yen	*Ilbon en* (Eel-bone inn) 일본 엔
Chinese currency	*Chungguk yuan* (Chuung-guuk yu-ahn) 중국 위엔
travelers' check	*yohangja supyo* (yuh-hang-jah supe-yoh-ruhl) 여행자 수표

What is the current exchange rate?
Dalleoeui hwanyuri otteoke twaeyo? (Dahl-lay-oh-we hwahn-yuu-ree aht-teh-oh-keh t'way-yoh?) 달러의 환율이 어떻게 되요?

Where can I change money?
Ton-eul odiso pakkweoyo? (Tone-yule ah-dee-soh pahk-kway-oh-yoh?) 돈을 어디서 바꿔요?

Do you accept travelers' checks?
Yohaengja supyo-rul pa ssumnikka? (Yuh-hang-jah suup-yoh-ruhl pah ssume-nee-kah?) 여행자 수표를 받습니까?

Please give me small change for this.
Chan don euro chuseyo (Chahn doan eh-uu-roh chuu-say-yoh) 잔돈으로 주세요.

48 Seasons *Kyejol* (Kay-juhl) 계절

spring	*pom* (pome) 봄	
in spring	*pom e* (pome eh) 봄에	
summer	*yorum* (yoh-rume) 여름	
in summer	*yorum e* (yoh-rume eh) 여름에	
fall	*kaul* (kah-uhl) 가을	
in fall	*kaul e* (kah-uhl eh) 가을에	
winter	*kyoul* (k'yoh-uhl) 겨울	
in winter	*kyoul e* (k'yoh-uhl eh) 겨울에	

49 The Weather *Nalsshi* (Nahl-she) 날씨

clouds	*kurum* (kuu-ruum) 구름
wind	*param* (pah-rahm) 바람
rain	*pi* (pee) 비
snow	*nun* (nuun) 눈
snow storm	*nun bora* (nuun boh-rah) 눈보라
typhoon	*taepung* (tay-puung) 태풍

cold	*chuun* (chuu-uun) 추운
ice	*orum* (uu-ruhm) 얼음
	aesu (aye-suu) 아이스
cool	*sonurhan* (suh-nur-hahn) 서늘한
warm	*dattutaeyo* (daht-tuh-tay-yoh) 따뜻해요
hot	*toun* (tah-uun) 더운
windy	*parami mani puroyo* (pah-rah-me mah-nee puu-ruh-yoh) 바람이 많이 불어요

How is the weather today?

Onul nalssinun otto ssumnikka? (Oh-nuhl nahl-she-nuun aht-toh sume-nee-kah?) 오늘 날씨는 이떻습니까?

It looks like rain, doesn't it?

Pi ga ol kot katchiyo? (Pee gah ohl kaht kaht-chee-yoh?) 비가 올 것 같지요?

It's awfully hot, isn't it!

Mopshi topkunyo! (Mope-she tup-kuun-yoh!) 몹시 덥군요!

It's raining!

Pi ga wayo! (Pee gah wah-yoh!) 비가 와요!

Do you think it will rain tomorrow?

Naeil pi ga ogessumnikka? (Nay-eel pee gah ah-gay-sume-nee-kah?) 내일 비가 오겠습니까?

It's snowing!

Nun-i wayo! (Nuun-ee wah-yoh!) 눈이 와요!

What is tomorrow's forecast?

Naeil ilgi yebonun? (Nay-eel eel-ghee yeh-buh-nuun?) 내일 일기 예보는?

* Please keep in mind that the hyphenated English phonetics should be pronounced in a smooth, even flow. Read them out loud several times to train your tongue and lips in making the proper sounds smoothly.

50 Airline / Airport *Hanggong hoesa* (Hahng-gong hway-sah) 항공 회사
Konghang (Kong-hahng) 공항

airline terminal 1	*che-il chongsa* (chuh-eel chohng-sah) 제 일 청사
airline terminal 2	*che-i chongsa* (chuh-ee chohng-sah) 제 이 청사
domestic terminal	*kungnae chongsa* (kuung-nay chohng-sah) 국내 청사

What time do I have to check in?
Myoshie chekuin-rul haeya dwaeyo? (Mwuh-she-eh check-in-ruhl hay-yah dway-yoh?) 몇시에 체크인을 해야되요?

How long does it take to fly to Chejudo Island?
Chejudo kaji olmana kollyo yo?
(Jeh-juu-do kah-jee ohl-mah-nah kohl-lay-oh-yoh?)
제주도까지 얼마나 걸려요?

Where is the departure gate?
Chulbalhanun tega odieyo? (Chuhl-bahl-hah-nuun deh-ga ah-dee-eh-yoh?) 출발하는 데가 어디에요?

51 Taxi(s) *Taekshi* (Tack-she) 택시

deluxe taxis	*mobom taekshi* (moh-buum tack-she) 모범 택시
jumbo (van) taxis	*chombo takeshi* (jum-boh tack-she) 점보 택시

Where can I catch a taxi?

Taekshi odiso chapchiyo? (Tahk-she ah-dee-soh chahp-chee-yoh?) 택시 어디서 잡지요?

Please call a taxi for me.

Taekshi-rul pullo chushio (Tahk-she-ruhl puhl-yoh chuu-she-oh) 택시를 불러주세요.

Please take me to the airport.

Ja-rul gong-hang-e diryada juseyo. (Jah-ruhl gohng-hahng-eh dee-r'yaw-dah juu-say-yoh) 저를 공항에 데려다 주세요.

How much does it cost to go to the airport by taxi?

Konghang-kka-ji taekshi yogom-i eolmayeyo? (Koong-hahng-kkah-jee tahk-she yoh-guum-ee eh-yohl-mah-yay-yoh?) 공항까지 택시요금이 얼마에요?

Please take me to the _____ hotel.

_____ *ho'tel kkaji kapshida* (_____ hotel kkah-jee kahp-she-dah) _____ 호텔까지 갑시다.

Take me to this address.

I chusoro chomka chuseyo (Ee chuu-soh-roh chome-kah chuu-say-yoh) 이 주소로 좀 가주세요.

Please wait for me.

Yogi-seo kidaryo chushigesseoyo (Yoh-ghee seh-oh kee-dah-rio chuu-she-gay-say-oh-yoh) 여기서 기다려 주시겠어요.

Please take me downtown.

Shinae chom ka chuseyo (She-nay chome kah chuu-say-yoh) 시내 좀 가주세요.

How much?

Eol mayeyo? (Eh-ohl mah-yay-oh?) 얼마예요?

*Regular taxis in Korea routinely pick up additional passengers who are going in the same general direction as their first passenger, in order to boost their income—a custom known as *hapsung* (hop-suung). The practice is illegal but widely carried out. People wanting a taxi shout out their destinations to drivers, who slow down when they see potential passengers waving at them. *Hapsung* is especially common during bad weather.

here *yogi* (yuh-ghee) 여기

Please stop here.
Yogi-seo sewo chuseyo (Yuh-ghee-say-oh say-woh chuu-say-yoh) 여기서 세워 주세요.

Please wait here.
Yogiso kidarishipshio (Yuh-ghee-suh kee-dah-ree-ship-she-oh) 여기서 기다리십시요.

hurry *soduruda* (suh-duu-ruh-dah) 서두르다

I'm in a hurry.
Na-nun soduru-go issumnida (Nah-nuun suh-duh-ruh-go e-sume-nee-dah) 나는 서두르고 있습니다.

there *kogi* (kuh-ghee) 거기

Please put the bag there.
Kabangul kogie noushio (Kah-bahng-uhl kuh-ghee-eh no-uh-she-oh) 가방을 거기에 놓으시오

left *wentchogui* (went-johg-we) 왼쪽의

Turn left at the next corner.
Taum motungieso wentchoguro toshio (Tah-uum moh-tuung-ee-eh-suh went-johg-uu-roh toh-she-oh) 다음 모퉁이에서 왼쪽으로 도시오

right *oruntchogui* (oh-ruhnt-johg-we) 오른쪽의

straight *ttokparun* (toke-pah-ruhn) 똑바른

Turn at the next corner.

Taum motung-i eso toseyo (Tah-uum moh-tuung-ee eh-suh toh-say-yoh) 다음 모퉁이에서 도세요

52 Subway *Chihachol* (Jee-hah-chuhl) 지하철

Subway lines in Korea are color-coded, with platform signs in Korean, English and Chinese characters. Many major stations are virtual art galleries, with public areas where people may meet friends, rest, read, etc.

subway station	*chihachol yok* (jee-hah-chuhl yuhk) 지하철역
ticket	*pyo* (p'-yoh) 표
ticket machine	*chapyo chadong panmaegi* (chahp-yoh chah-dohng pahn-may-ghæe) 차표 자동 판매기
ticket office	*maepyo so* (mape-yoh soh) 매표소
ticket window	*maepyo gu* (mape-yoh-guu) 매표구

Where is a subway station?

Chihachol yok-i odiso yo? (Jee-hah-chuhl yuhk-ee ah-dee-suh yoh?) 지하철 역이 어딨어요?

Do you have a subway map in English?

Yong-o-ro toen chihachol chidoga isseoyo? (Yuhng-oh roh toh-un chee-hah-chohl chee-doh-gah ees-say-oh-yoh?) 영어로 된 지하철 지도가 있어요?

Where should I get off to go to _____?

_____ *e-karyo myon odiso naeryeo-ya twaeyo?* (_____ eh-kah-rio m'yohn ah-dee-sah nay-ray-oh-yah tway-yoh?) _____ 에 가려면 어디서 내려야되요?

How much is the fare?

Yogum un olmaimnikka? (Yoh-guum uhn ohl-my-mm-nee-kah?) 요금은 얼마입니까?

Where can I buy a ticket?
P'yo odiso salsu issoyo? (P'yoh ah-dee-sah sahl-suu ee-sah-yoh?) 표 어디서 살 수 있어요?

53 Bus *Bosu* (Buh-suu) 버스

1st class metro bus	*chwa sok bosu* (chwah soak buh-suu) 좌석버스
regular metro bus	*shinae bosu* (she-nay buh-suu) 시내버스
inter-city bus	*kan-sun bosu* (kang-suu buh-suu) 간선버스
town, village bus	*chikaeng bosu* (jee-kang buh-suu) 직행버스
neighborhood bus	*maul bosu* (mah-uhl buh-suu) 마을버스
bus stop	*bosu jongryujang* (buh-suu johng-rue-jahng) 버스 정류장
express bus	*kosok bosu* (koh-soak buh-suu) 고속버스
sightseeing bus	*kwangwang bosu* (kwahn-gwahng buh-suu) 관광버스
prepaid electronic transit pass	*kyotong kadu* (k'yoh-tong kah-duu) 교통카드

Is there a bus stop near here?
I kuchoe bosu chongnyujangi issumnikka? (Ee kuu-choh-eh buh-suu chohng-nyuu-jahn-ghee e-sume-nee-kah?) 이 근처에 버스 정류장이 있습니까?

Is there a bus to downtown?
Toshimji-ro kanun bosu pyoni issumnika? (Toh-sheem-jee-roh kah-nuun buh-suu p'yoh-nee e-sume-nee-kah?) 도심지로 가는 버스편이 있습니까?

How often do buses run?

Bosu ga myoppunmada wayo? (Buh-suu gah m'yahp-puun-mah-dah wah-yoh?) 버스가 몇 분마다 와요?

Which bus goes to _____?

Myoppon bosu ga _____ e kayo? (M'yahp-puun buh-suu ga _____ eh kah-yoh?) 몇 번 버스가 ____ 에가요?

Please let me off here.

Naeryo juseyo (Nay-rio juu-say-yoh) 내려주세요.

54 Cars *Jadongcha* (Jah-dong-chah) 자동차

driver	*unjonsu* (uun-chone-suu) 운전수
driver's license	*unjon myonhojung* (uun-juhn m'yuhn-huh-juung) 운전면허증
parking lot	*jucha jang* (juu-chah jahng) 주차장
no parking	*jucha jeumji* (juu-chah jome-jee) 주차 금지
service station	*jadongcha juyuso* (jah-dong-chah juu-yuu-sah) 자동차 주유소
speed limit	*sokto jehan* (soak-toh jay-hahn) 속도 제한
insurance	*pohom* (poh-home) 보험

I would like to rent a car.

Cha-rul piligo shipssmnida. (Chah-ruhl pee-lee-go ship-sume-nee-dah) 차를 빌리고 싶습니다.

Where can I rent a car?

Odiso cha rentu halsu issoyo? (Ah-dee-sah chah ren-tuu hahl-suu ee-sah-yoh?) 어디서 차 렌트 할 수 있어요?

I also want a driver.

Yokshi unjosu piryo hamnida. (Yuk-she uun-joh-suu ga pee-rio hahm-nee-dah) 역시 운전수가 필요합니다.

How much by the day?

Harue olmaeyo? (Hah-ruu-eh uhl-may-yoh?) 하루에 얼마에요?

55 Trains *Kicha* (Kee-chah) 기차

express train	*saemaul-ho* (say-mahl-hoh) 새마을호
semi-express	*mugunghwa-ho* (muu-guung-hwah-hoh) 무궁화호
local stops	*tong-il-ho* (tohng-eel-hoh) 통일호
conductor	*chajang* (chah-jahng) 차장
one-way ticket	*pyondo pyo* (p'yohn-doh) 편도표
round-trip ticket	*wanbok pyo* (wahn-boak p'yoh) 왕복표
student ticket	*haksang pyo* (hahk-sang p'yoh) 학생표
senior citizen's ticket	*noin/kyongno pyo* (noh-een k'yohng p'yoh) 노인 / 경노표
first-class seat	*il-dung sok* (eel-duung-suk) 일등석
second-class seat	*i-dung sok* (ee-duung suk) 이등석
standing room ticket	*ip sok* (eep suk) 입석
dining car	*shiktang cha* (sheek-tahng chah) 식당차

Is this the train for Pusan?

Pusan hang yol cha-e yoh? (Buu-sahn hang yohl chah-eh yoh?) 부산행 열차예요?

Two tickets to Pusan, please.

Pusan hang pi-hang-gi pyo-rul tu chang chuseyo (Buu-sahn hang pee-hang-ghee p'yoh-ruhl tuu chahng chuu-say-yoh) 부산행 비행기표를 두 장 주세요.

What number is the dining car?
Shiktang cha-nun myopon imnikka? (Sheek-tahng chah-nuun myah-puhn eem-nee-kkah?) 식당차는 몇 번입니까?

sleeping car *chimdae cha* (cheem-day chah) 침대차

What number is the sleeping car?
Chimdae cha-nun myoppon imnikka? (Cheem-day chah-nuun m'yahp-puhn eem-nee-kkah?) 침대차는 몇번입니까?

What station is this?
Yogi-ga musun yogie yo? (Yuu-ghee-gah muu-suhn yuu-ghee-eh yoh?) 여기가 무슨 역이에요?

What is the next station?
Taum yogi odie yo? (Tah-uum yu-ghee ah-dee-eh yoh?) 다음 역이 어디에요?

I want to get off at Taegu.
Taegu eso naeriryogo hanun deyo (Tay-guu eh-suh nay-ree-r'yoh-go hah-nuun day-yoh) 대구에서 내리려고 하는데요

56 Bathroom / Toilet *Hwajangshil* (Hwah-jahang-sheel) 화장실

American-style bathroom	*Yokshil* (Yoke-sheel) 욕실
lavatory	*Pyonso* (Pyun-soh) 변소
flush toilet	*suseshik pyonso* (suu-say-sheek pyun-soh) 수세식 변소
toilet paper	*hyuji* (hugh-jee) 휴지
public bathhouse	*mokyok tang* (moke-yoke-tahng) 목욕탕

Where is a/the restoom?

Hwajang-shil-i odi issoyo? (Hwah-jahng sheel-ee ah-dee-saw?) 화장실이 어디 있어요?

Where is a/the toilet?

Pyonso ga odi imnikka? (Pyun-soh gah ah-dee eem-nee-kah?) 변소가 어디 입니까?

57 Hotels *hot'el* (hoh-tel) 호텔

guesthouse	*minbakchip* (meen-bahk-cheep) 민박집
motel	*motel / yogwan* (yuh-gwahn) 모텔
family-run bed-and-breakfast type facilities	*minbak* (meen-bahk) 민박
reservations	*yeyak* (yay-yahk) 예약
to confirm	*hwaginhada* (hwah-geen-hah-dah) 확인하다
room	*pang* (pahng) 방
room charge	*pang kap* (pahng kahp) 방값
room number	*pang ponho* (pahng bahn-hoh) 방번호
room key	*pang yolsweo* (pahng yahl-swah) 방열쇠
single bed	*ilinyong chimdae* (eel-een-yong cheem-day) 일인용 침대
double bed	*iinyong chimdae* (e-een-yong cheem-day) 이인용 침대
front desk	*chop sugyee* (chup suu-geh-eh) 접수계
bell boy	*poi* (boy) 보이
maid	*ajumma* (ah-juum-mah) 아줌마
bath	*mogyok tang* (moag-yoke tahng) 목욕탕
shower	*swawoe* (sha-wah) 샤워

inn (Korean)	*yogwan* (yuh-gwahn) 여관
hotel taxi	*hotel taekshi* (hoh-tel tack-she)
	호텔 택시

Can I pay with a credit card?

Kureditu kadu-ro kyesan dwae yo?
(Kuu-ray-dee-tuu kah-duu- roh keh-sahn dway yoh?)
크레디트 카드로 계산되요?

Do you take travelers' checks?

Yohaeng-ja supyo pada yo? (Yuh-hang-jah suup-yoh pah-
dah yoh?) 여행자 수표 받아요?

58 Eating *Mokta* (Muhk-tah) 먹다

(Polite form of to eat) *Chapsuda* (Chahp-suu-dah) 잡수다

breakfast	*achim* (ah-cheem) 아침
lunch	*chomshim* (chume-sheem) 점심
dinner	*chonyok* (chune-yuuk) 저녁
side dishes	*pan chan* (pahn chahn) 반찬
menu	*menyu* (meh-nyuu) 메뉴

I'm hungry.

Chonun paego p'ayo (Chuh-nuun pay-goh pah-yoh)
저는 배 고파요

I would like to eat Chinese food.

Chungguk-shik-rul mokko shipundeyo (Chuung-guuk-
sheek-ruhl moke-koh ship-uhn-deh-yoh)
중국식을 먹고 싶은데요.

Do you have a menu in English?

Yong-o-ro doen menu issoyo? (Yung-uu-roh doh-en men-
yuu ee-suh-yoh?) 영어로 된 메뉴 있어요?

| waiter | *weita* (way-tah) 웨이타 |

waitress	*weituresu* (waitress) 웨이트레스
Korean food	*Hanguk yori* (Hahn-guuk yoh-ree) 한국 요리
Chinese food	*Chungguk yori* (Chuung-guuk yoh-ree) 중국 요리
Western food	*Soyang yori* (Sah-yahng yoh-ree) 서양 요리
Japanese food	*Ilbon yori* (Eel-bone yoh-ree) 일본 요리
spicy	*maeun* (may-uun) 매운
fork	*poku* (poh-kuu / foh-kuu) 포크
knife	*naipu* (nie-puh / nie-fuu) 나이프
spoon	*sukkarak* (suuk-kah-rahk) 숟가락
chopsticks	*chokkarak* (chuuk-kah-rahk) 젓가락
toothpick	*issushigae* (ee-suu-she-gay) 이쑤시개
bread	*pang* (pahng) 빵
rice (cooked)	*pap* (pahp) 밥
chicken	*takkogi* (tahk-koh-ghee) 닭고기
eggs	*talgyal* (tahl-g'yahl) 달걀
fish	*saengson* (sang-suhn) 생선
broiled fish	*saengson gui* (sang-sahn gway) 생선 구이
pork	*twaejigogi* (tway-jee-go-ghee) 돼지구이
pork ribs	*twaejigal bi* (tway-jee-gahl bee) 돼지 갈비
beef ribs	*pulgal bi* (buhl-gahl bee) 불갈비
roast beef	*pulgogi* (buhl-go-ghee) 불고기
noodles with meat and vegetables	*chap chae* (chop-chay) 잡채
skewered beef and vegetables	*san jeok* (sahn joak) 산적
vegetables	*yachae* (yah-chay) 야채
side dishes	*pan chan* (pahn chahn) 반찬

Please start (eating).
Chapsuseyo (Chop-suu-say-yoh) 잡수세요

Just a little, please.
Chogum, juseyo (Choh-guhm, juu-say-yoh) 조금주세요

Is this dish spicy?
I umshing maewoyo? (Ee uhm-sheeng may-woh-yoh?)
이 음식 매워요?

Please bring me a fork.
Poku-rul katta chushipshio (Poh-kuu-ruhl kaht-tah chuu-ship-she-oh) 포크를 갖다주십시요.

(Bring me some) bread, please.
pang, chushipshio (Pahng, chuu-ship-she-oh) 빵 주십시요.

59 Drinks *Umnyo* (Uhm-n'yoh) 음료

To drink *Mashida* (Mah-she-dah) 마시다

alcoholic drink	*sul* (suhl) 술
soft drink	*chong-nyang umnyo* (chohng-n'yahng uum-n'yoh) 청량음료
bar (for drinking)	*ppa* (bah) 바
bar snacks	*anju* (ahn-juu)* 안주

*Some bars require that patrons automatically accept side dishes of *anju* as a kind of cover charge.

cabaret (with hostesses)	*k'yabare* (k'yah-bah-ray) 캬바레
hostess	*hosutesu* (hos-teh-suu) 호스테스
hostess fee	*hosutesu tip* (hos-teh-suu teep) 호스테스 팁
	kisaeng (kee-sang)* 기생

55

Kisaeng are the Korean equivalent of Japan's geisha. However, they predated geisha by some one thousand years.

kisaeng house   *kisaeng jip* (kee-sang jeep) 기생집
karaoke place   *norae bang* (no-ray bahng) 노래방
literally "song room"

I'm thirsty.

Chonun mongmallayo (Chuh-nuun mong-mahl-lah-yoh)
저는 목 말라요.

What are you doing this evening?

Onulbame mwo haseyo? (Oh-nuhl-bah-meh mwah hah-say-yoh?) 오늘밤에 뭐하세요?

Let's have a drink.

Muot jom mashipshida (Mwaht johm mah-ship-she-dah)
뭣 좀 마십시다.

Let's go to a cabaret.

Kyabare ro kapshida (K'yah-bah-ray roh kahp-she-dah)
캬바레로 갑시다.

What time shall we meet?

Myoshie mannalkkayo? (Myuh-she-eh mahn-nahl-kah-yoh?) 몇시에 만날까요?

water	*mul* (muhl) 물;	
bottled water	*saengsu* (sang-suu) 생수;	
mineral water	*yakssu* (yahk-suu) 약수	
coffee	*kopi* (koh-pee) 커피	
coffee shop	*kopi shyop* (koh-pee shyop) 커피숍	
black tea	*hong cha* (hong chah) 홍차	
ginseng tea	*insam cha* (een-sahm chah) 인삼 차	
milk	*uyu* (uu-yuu) 우유	
cocktail	*kakteil* (cocktail) 칵테일	
beer	*maekchu* (make-juu) 맥주;	
	pio (bee-ah) 비어	

| **whisky** | *wisuki* (whis-kee) 위스키 |
| **wine** | *podoju* (buh-doh-juu) 포도주 |

makkoli (mahk-koh-lee) 막걸리: an inexpensive milky wine made from rice and barley; the working man's drink for a long time.

makkoli jip (mahk-koh-lee jeep) 막걸리 집: a bar or tavern specializing in this drink.

Water, please.
Mul, chushipshio (Muhl, chuu-ship-she-oh) 물 주십시오.

Coffee, please.
Kopi, chushipshio (Koh-pee, chuu-ship-she-oh) 커피 주십시오.

Beer, please.
Pio, chushipshio (Bee-ah, chuu-ship-she-oh) 표 주십시오.

Is there a cover charge?
Ip jjang nyo ga issoyo? (Eep jahng n'yoh gah ee-soh-yoh?) 입장료가 있어요?

Cheers! *Konbae!* (Kom-bay!) 건배!

60 Bill / Receipt *Kyesanso* (Kay-sahn-suh) / *Yongsujung* (Yuung-suu-juung) 영수증

Please bring me my bill.
Kyesanso-rul kajo oshio (Kay-sahn-suh-ruhl kah-joh ah-she-oh) 계산서를 가져 오시오.

Let me pay the bill.
Kyesan-un naega hagessumnida (Kay-sahn-uun nay-gah hah-gay-sume-nee-dah) 계산은 내가 하겠습니다.

Come on, I'm paying!
Cha, naega sagessumnida! (Chah, nay-gah sah-geh-sume-nee-dah!) 자, 내가 사겠습니다!

A receipt, please.
Yongsujung-ul chuseyo (Yuung-suu-juung-uhl chuu-say-yoh) 영수증을 주세요.

61 Telephone *Chonwha* (Chune-whah) 전화

public telephone	*kongjung chonhwa* (kong-juung chune-whah) 공중전화
house phone	*jeonwha* (jone-whah) 전화
telephone number	*chonhwa ponho* (chune-hwah bahn-hoh) 전화번호
telephone directory	*chonhwa ponhobu* (chune-whah bahn-hoe-buu) 전화번호부
overseas call	*kukje chonwha* (kuuk-jay chune-whah) 국제전화
long distance call	*shioe chonwha* (she-oh-eh chune-whah) 시외전화

Where is a public phone?
Kongjung chonhwa ga issoyo? (Kohng-juung chune-whah-gah ee-suh-yoh?) 공중전화가 있어요?

I want to make a local call.
Shinae chonhwa-rul hago shippundeyo (She-nay chune-whah-ruhl hah-go ship-puun-day-yoh) 시내 전화를 하고 싶은데요.

I want to make an international call.
Kukjje chonhwa rul hago shippundeyo (Kuuk-jay chune-whah ruhl hah-go ship-puun-day-yoh) 국제젠화를 하고 싶은데요.

I want to make a collect call.
Sushin-in chibul chonhwa (Suu-sheen een chee-buhl chune-whah) 수신인 지불 전화.

May I have your phone number?
Chonwha ponho rul chushigesseoyo? (Chune-whah bohn-hoh ruhl chuu-she-geh-say-oh-yoh?) 전화번호를 주시겠어요?

62 Cell Phone *Handu pon* (Hahn-duu pon) 핸드폰

I would like to rent a cell phone.
Hand phone-rul pilligo shipsumnida (Hah-duu fohn-ruhl peel-lee-go ship-sume-nee-dah) 핸드폰을 빌리고 싶습니다.

I want to buy a cell phone.
Hand phone-rul sago shipsumnida (Hahn-duu fohn-ruhl sah-go ship-sume-nee-dah) 핸드폰을 사고 싶습니다.

63 Computer *Kompyuto* (Kohm-pyuu-tah) 컴퓨터

I'd like to use a computer.
Kompyuto-rul ssugo shipundeyo (Kome-pyuu-tuh-ruhl suh-go she-puun-day-yoh) 컴퓨터를 쓰고 싶은데요.

May I borrow a computer?
Kompyuto chom pillyo chushigessum nikka? (Kohm-pyuu-tah chome peel-l'uuh chuu-she-guh-sume nee-kkah?) 컴퓨터를 좀 빌려주시겠습니까?

Where can I plug in my laptop?
Che notubugul yon-gyohalsu innun goshi issoyo? (Cheh no-tu-buuk-uhl yun gulh-hahl-suu een-nuhn go-she ee-suh-yoh?) 제 노트북을 연결할 수 있는 곳이 있어요?

64 **Internet** *Intonet* (In-tah-net-tu) 인터넷

Internet café	*Intonet kape* (In-ter-net-tu kah-pay) 인터넷 카페
Also:	*Pishi-Bang* (pee-she bahng) 피시방 literally, PC room
modem	*moden* 모뎀

65 **Email** *Imeil* (Ee-mail) 이메일

I'd like to send an email.
Imeil-rul ponaeryogo hanundeyo
(Ee-mail-ruhl poh-nay-re-yoh-guh hah-nuun-day-yoh)
이메일을 보내려고 하는데요.

I'd like to check my email.
Imeil hwagin haryogo hanundeyo
(E-mail hwah-geen hah-re-yoh-guh hah-nuun-day-yoh)
이메일 확인하려고 하는데요.

What is your email address?
Emeil chuso-ga ottoke dwae yo?
(Ee-mail juu-suh-gah uht-tuh-kay dway yoh?)
이메일 주소가 어떻게 되요?

66 **Shopping** *Syoping* (shope-peeng) 쇼핑

shopping center	*syoping sento* (shope-peeng sentah) 쇼핑 센터
shop (store)	*kage* (kah-gay) 가게
department store	*paekhwa jom* (pake-whah jome) 백화점
open-air market	*shijang* (she-jahng) 시장
South Gate Market (Seoul)	*Namdaemun Shijang* (Nahm-day-muun She-jahng) 남대문 시장

East Gate Market (Seoul)	*Tongdaemun Shijang* (Tohng-day-muun She-jahng) 동대문 시장
gift shop	*kinyom pum sang* (kee-yome pume sahng) 기념품상
tax-free goods	*myon-se pum* (m'yone-say pume) 면세품
price	*taeka* (tay-kah) 대가; *kagyok* (kahg-yoke) 가격
receipt	*yongsujung* (yohng-sue-juung) 영수증
drugstore	*yakkuk* (yahk-kuuk) 약국
credit card	*kuredit kadu* (kuu-reh-deet kah-duu) 크레디트 카드
Visa Card	*Pija Kadu* (Bee-jah Kah-duu) 비자 카드
Master Card	*Masuta Kadu* (Mahs-tah Kah-duu) 마스타 카드

I want to go shopping.

Syoping kago shipsumnida (Shope-peeng kah-go ship-sume-nee-dah) 쇼핑 가고 싶습니다

Where is the nearest department store?

Cheil kakkaun paekwa jom i odi issoyo? (Chale kahk-kah-uun pake-wah juhm i ad-dee ee-suh-yoh?) 제일 가까운 백화점이 어디있어요?

Where is the nearest (open air) market?

Cheil kakkaun shijang ga odi issoyo? (Chale kahk-kah-uun she-jahng ad-dee ee-suh-yoh?) 제일 가까운 시장이 어디있어요?

Where is the nearest craft shop?

Cheil kakkaun kongyepum kage? Ga odi issoyo? (Chale kahk-kah-uun kong-yeh-puum kah-gay?) 제일 가까운 공예품 가게가 어디 있어요?

I'm tired.
Pigon haeyo (Pee-gohn hay-yoh) 피곤해요.

Let's take a rest.
Chom shwipshida (Chome shweep she-dah) 좀 쉽시다.

67 Bargain Sales *Pagen Seil* (Bah-gane Sale) 바겐 세일

Are there any bargain sales going on now?
Chigum pagen seil hanun koshi issumnikka? (Chee-guhm bah-gane sale hah-nuun koh-she ee-sume-nee-kah?) 지금 바겐세일 하는 곳이 있습니까?

Are you having a bargain sale?
Chigum pagen seil hanun chung imnika? (Chee-guum bah-gane sale hah-nuun chuung eem-nee-kah?) 지금 바겐 세일 하는 중입니까?

68 Discount *Harin* (hah-reen) 할인; *Enuri* (Ee-nuu-ree) 에누리

That price is too high!
Nomu pissayo! (No-muu pee-sah-yoh!) 너무 비싸요!

Can you give me a discount?
Harinhae chushigessumnikka? (Hah-reen-hay chuu-she-guh-sume-nee-kah?) 할인해 주시겠습니까?

I'll give you _____ .
_____ *durilkkeyo*
(_____ duh-reel-keh-yoh) 드릴께요.

Do you have anything cheaper?
Tossan gotto issoyo? (Tuh-sahn gut-toh ee-suh-yoh?) 더 싼 것도 있어요?

central post office	*jungang uche guk* (juun-ahng uu-cheh guuk) 중앙우체국
international parcel post office	*kukje sopo uche guk* (kuuk-jay sope-oh uu-cheh guuk) 국제 소포 우체국
letter	*pyonji* (pyahn-jee) 편지
postage	*uphyon yogum* (uu-pyahn yoh-guhm) 우편 요금
stamp	*uphyo* (uu-pyah) 우표
airmail	*hanggong uphyon* (hahng-goon uu-pyahn) 항공 우표
surface mail	*sonbak uphyon* (sahn-bahk uu-pyuhn) 선박 우표
foreign mail	*oegug uphyon* (way-guug uu-pyuhn) 외국 우표
registered mail	*tunggi uphyon* (tuung-ghee uu-pyuhn) 등기우표
express mail	*soktal* (soak-tahl) 속달
parcel post	*sop'o* (sope-oh) 소포
printed matter	*inswae mul* (en-sway-muhl) 인쇄물
address	*juso* (juu-soh) 주소
return address	*palshinin juso* (pahl-sheen-een juu-soh) 발신인 주소
P.O. Box	*Sa Seo Ham* (Sah Say-oh Hahm) 사서함
envelope	*pongtu* (pong-tuu) 봉투

I want to mail a letter.

Pyonji-rul puchigo (P'yohn-jee ruhl puu-chee-go) 편지를 부치고

Where can I get this wrapped?

Pojang-ha nun tega eodi isseoyo? (Poh-jahng ha nuun tay-gah ah-dee ees-say-oh-yoh?) 포장하는 데가 어디 있어 요?

Health *Konggang* (Kuung-gahng) 건강

allergy	*allerugi* (ahl-ehh-ruh-ghee) 알레르기
appendicitis	*maengjangyom* (mang-jahng-yuhm) 맹장염
cough	*kichimul haeyo* (kee-chee-muhl hay-yoh) 기침을 해요
diarrhea	*solsa* (suhl-sah) 설사
food poisoning	*shik chungdo-ge kollyossoyo* (sheek chuung-doh-gay kuhl-lyuh-ssuh-yoh) 식중독에 걸렸어요
hay fever	*konchoyori issoyo* (kuhn-choh-yuh-ree ee-ssuh-yoh) 고초열이있어요
headache	*tudong* (tuu-tohng) 두통
heart	*shimjang* (sheem-jahng) 심장
heart attack	*shimjang mabi* (sheem-jahng mah-bee) 심장마비
high fever	*koyol* (koh-yuhl) 고열

71 **Ill / Sick** *Pyongnan* (P'yohng-nahn) 병단

any doctor	*uisa* (we-sah) 의사
female doctor	*yoja uisa* (yuh-jah we-sah) 여자의사

I feel (am) sick.
Momi apumnida (Moh-me ah-pume-nee-dah)
몸이 아픕니다.

I'm sick.
Pyong-i nasseoyo (P'yohng-ee nahs-say-oh-yoh)
병이 났어요.

I've got a bad cold.
Na-nu shimhan kamgie kollyossumnida (Nah-nuu sheem-hahn kahm-ghee-eh kohl-yuh sume-nee-dah)
나는 심한 감기에 걸렸습니다.

(I have) diarrhea.
Solsahada (Suhl-sah-hah-dah) 설사하다.

I have a bad headache.
Nanun tutong-i maeu shimhamnida
(Nah-nuun tuu-dohng ee may-uu sheem-hahm-nee-dah)
나는 두통이 매우 심합니다.

Please send for a doctor.
Uisa-rul pulro chuseyo (We-sah-ruhl puhl-roh chuu-say-yoh) 의사를 불러주세요.

Dr. Kim	*Kim Pakssa* (Kim Pahk-ssah)	김박사
nurse	*kanhosa* (kahn-hoh-sah)	간호사
hospital	*pyongwon* (p'yuung-wun)	병원
pharmacy	*yakkuk* (yahk-kuuk)	약국

72 Dentist *Chikkwauisa* (Cheek-kwah-ee-sah) 치과의사

toothache	*chitong-i issoyo* (chee-tohng-ee ee-ssuh-yoh) 치통이 있어요

I have a toothache.
Nanun iga apayo (Nah-nuun ee-gah ah-pah-yoh)
나는 이가 아파요.

I've lost a filling.
Pong-i bajo ssoyo (Pong-ee bah-juh suh-yoh)
봉이 빠졌어요.

I need to go to a dentist.
Chikwae kago chipssumnida (Cheek-kway kah-go chip-sume-nee-dah) 치과에 가고 싶습니다.

Do you know a dentist who speaks English?

Yong-o rul malha-nun chikwauisa-rul ashimnikka?
(Yohng-ah ruhl mahl-hah-nuun chee-kwa-we-sah-ruhl ah-
sheem-nee-kah?) 영어를 말하는 치과의사를 아십니
까?

I want to make an appointment with the dentist.

Ku chikkwa-e ye yak-ul hago shipundeyo (Kuu cheek-
wah-eh yahk-ruhl hah-go ship-uhn-deh-yoh) 그 치과에
예약을 하고싶은데요.

73 Emergencies *Pisang Sangtae* (Pee-sahng Sang-tay)

ambulance	*ambyullonsu* (ambulance) 앰뷸런스; *kugupcha* (kuu-guup-chah) 구급차
injury (wound)	*pusang* (puu-sahng) 부상
cut, bruise	*sangcho* (sahng-choh) 상처
severe wound	*chung sang* (chuung sahng) 중상
help! (call for)	*towa chuseyo!* (toh-wah chuu-say-yoh!) 도와주세요!
heart attack	*shimjang mabi* (sheem-jahng mah-bee) 심장마비
emergency exit	*pisang gu* (pee-sahng guu) 비상구

I've been hurt!

Chega tacho sseo yo! (Chay-gah tah-choh say-oh yoh!)
제가 다쳤어요!

Please call an ambulance!

Kugupcha chom pullol chuseyo! (Kuu-guup-chah chome
puhl-yohl chuu-say-yoh!) 구급차 좀 불러주세요!

Please call an ambulance quickly!

Ppalli kugupcha rul pullo chuseyo!
(Bahl-lee kuu-guup-chah ruhl puhl-lah chuu-say-yoh!)
빨리 구급차를 불러 주세요!

I am disabled.
Chon chang-aein indeyo (Chohn chahng-aa-een een-day-yoh) 전 장애인 인데요.

Is there wheelchair access?
Hwilcheo churipkuga issoyo? (Wheel cheh-ah chuu-reep-kuu-gah ee-ssuh-yoh?) 휠체어 출입구가 있어요?

Fire! (shout in case of fire)
Puriya! (Buu-ree-yah!) 불이야!

Help! (shout in a life-threatening situation)
Towa juseyo! (Doh-wah juu-say-yoh!) 도와 주세요!

Watch out! (when danger threatens)
Choshim haeyo! (Choh-sheem hay-yoh!) 조심해요!

I'm lost!
Ki-rul irossoyo! (Kee-ruhl ee-ruh-ssuh-yoh!)
길을 잃었어요!

Would you please help me?
Chom towa chushige sumnikka? (Chome tow-wah chuu-she-geh sume-nee-kah? 좀 도와 주시겠습니까?

May I use your telephone?
Chonhwa chom sseodo doelkkayo? (Chune-whah chome show-doh dohl-kah yoh?) 전화 좀 써도 될까요?

74 Barbershop *ibalsso* (ee-bahl-ssah) 이발소

barber /   *ibalsa* (ee-bahl-sah) 이발사
  hair dresser
haircut   *ibal* (ee-bahl) 이발

Is there a barbershop in the hotel?
Hotel-e ibalsso-ga issumnikka? (Hotel eh ee-bahl-ssah-ga ee-sume-nee-kah?) 호텔에 이발소가 있습니까?

How much for a haircut?
Iballyo ga olma imnikka? (Ee-bahl-lyoh-gah ahl-mah eem-nee-kah?) 이발료 가 얼마 입니까?

Just a trim, please.
Chogum man kka-kka chuseyo (Choh-guum mahn kah-kah chuu-say-yoh) 조금만 깍아주세요.

75 Beauty Salon *Mijang won* (Me-jahng wahn) 미장원

hair set	*mori-rul setu* (muh-ree-ruhl say-tuu) 머리를 세트
shampoo	*shyampu* (shahm-puu) 샴푸

Is there a beauty salon in the hotel?
Hotel-e mijang won i issumnikka? (Hotel eh me-jahng wahn i ee-sume-nee-kah?) 호텔에 미장원이 있습니까?

I would like to have my hair set.
Morirul setuhae chushipshio (Muh-ree-ruhl say-tuu-hay chuu-ship-she-oh) 머리를 세트해 주십시오.

A shampoo, please.
Shyampu, chushipshio (Shahm-puu chuu-ship-she-oh) 샴푸 주십시오.

76 Sightseeing *kwangwang* (kwahn-gwahng) 관광; *kugyong* (kuu-g'yohng) 구경

sightseeing bus	*kwangwang bosu* (kwahn-gwahng buh-suu) 관광버스
tourist information office	*kwangwang annaeso* (kwahn gwahn ahn-nay-soh) 관광 안내소
Korean Folk Village	*Minsok Chon* (Meen-soak Chuhn) 민속촌

far   **mon** (mun) 먼; *molli* (muhl-lee)
멀리

I want to go sightseeing.
Kwangwang hago shipsupnida (Kwahn-gwahng hah-go ship-suup-nee-dah) 관광하고 싶습니다.

Where is a/the tourist information office?
Kwangwang annaeso-i ga odi isso yo? (Kwahn-gwahn ahn-nay-ee gah ah-dee ee-suh yoh?) 관광 안내소 가 어 디 있어요?

How far is it from here?
Yogiso olmana momnika? (Yuh-ghee-suh ohl-mah-nah mum-nee-kah?) 여기서 얼마나 멉니까?

How long does the trip take?
Olmana yonchak dwaeyo? (Ohl-mah-nah yuhn-chack dway-yoh?) 얼마나 연착되요?

Can I take a bus to the Korean Folk Village?
Minsok Chon-e pposeo-ro kal su issoyo? (Meen-soak Chohn-eh poh-suh-roh kahl suu ee-suh-yoh?) 민속촌에 버스로 갈 수 있어요?

Can I go to Cheju Island by ferry?
Cheju Do hang peri-ga issoyo? (Cheh-juu Doh hang pay-ree-gah ee-soh-yoh?) 제주도행 페리가 있어요?

77 Folk Customs *Pungsup* (Puung-suhp) 풍습

folk dance	*minsok muyong* (meen-soak muu-yohng) 민속 무용
Korean folk songs	*Hanguk minyo* (Hahn-guuk meen-yoh) 한국 민요
crane dance	*hak chum* (hahk chuum) 학춤
monk's dance	*sung-mu* (suhg-muu) 승무

I'm interested in the drum dance.

Changgo chum-e kwanshim-i isseo yo (Chahng-go chuum-eh kwahn-sheem-ee ee-say-oh yoh) 장고춤에 관심이 있어요.

What is playing at the Sejong Cultural Center?

Sejong Munwha Hogwan-e seo musun kongyon-i isseoyo? (Say-johng Muun-whah Hoh-gwahn-eh say-oh muu-suun kong yohn-ee ee-say-oh yoh?) 세종문화회관에서 무슨 공연이 있어요?

I would like to have a recording of Korean folk songs.

Hanguk minyo rekodu-rul han chang sago shipsumnida (Hahn-guuk meen-yoh ray-koh-duu-ruhl hahn chahng sah-go ship-sume-nee-dah) 한국 민요레코드를 한 장 사고 싶습니다.

Is this a Korean custom?

Igosun Hanguk pungsup imnikka? (Ee-go-suun Hahn-guuk puung-suhp eem-nee-kah?) 이것은 한국 풍습입니까?

78 Admission *Ipchang* (Eep-chahng) 입장

admission fee *ipchang nyo* (eep-chahng n'yoh) 입장료

admission ticket *ipchang kwon* (eep-chahng kwun) 입장권

What is the admission fee?

Ipchang nyo-ga olma imnika? (Eep-chanhng n'yoh gah ahl-mah eem-nee-kah?) 입장료가 얼마입니까?

Is it free?

Muryo imnikka? (Muu-rio eem-nee-kah?) 무료입니까?

79 Great South Gate* *Namdaemun* (Nahm-day-muun) 남대문

*Seoul's most famous gate, ranked as Korea's National Treasure Number 1.

I would like to go to Namdaemun.
Namdaemun-e kago shipsumneda (Nahm-day-muun-eh kah-go ship-sume-nee-dah) 남대문에 가고 싶습니다.

Please take me to Namdaemun.
Namdaemun-eu-ro chom kachuseyo (Nahm-day-muun-yuu-roh chome kah-chuu-say-yoh) 남대문으로 좀 가주세요.

80 The Blue House* *Chongwa Dae* (Chohng-wah Day) 청와대

*The President's Residence

Where is the Blue House?
Chongwa Dae-ga odiso soh-yoh? (Chohng-wah Day-gah ad-dee-suh soh-yoh?) 청와대가 어딨어요?

Is the Blue House open to visitors?
Chongwa Dae reul ku-gyong-hal reul su issoyo? (Chohng-wah Day ruhl kuu-gyohng-hahl suu ee-soh-yoh?) 청와대를 구경할 수 있어요?

81 Panmunjom *Panmunjom* (Pahn-muun-jome) 판문점 (The DMZ Command Grounds)

I would like to go to Panmunjom.
Panmunjom-e ka-go shipoyo (Pahn-muun-jome-e kah-go ship-oh-yoh) 판문점에 가고 싶어요.

How far is it from here?

Yogiso olmana momnikka? (Yuh-ghee-suh ohl-mah-nah mum-nee-kah?) 여기서 얼마나 멉니까?

82 Avenue / Street *Toro* (Doh-roh) 도로

What is the name of this street?

I toro-e irumi mwoshimnika? (Ee doh-roh-eh ee-ruu-me mwah-sheem-nee-kah?) 이 도로의 이름이 무엇입니까?

83 Sports *Undong* (Uhn-dong) 운동

baseball	*yagu* (yah-guu)	야구
basketball	*nonggu* (nong-guu)	농구
golf	*kolpu* (kohl-puu)	골프
ice hockey	*aisu haki* (aye-suu hah-kee) 아이스 하키	
martial arts	*musul* (muu-suhl)	무술
soccer	*chukku* (chuhk-kuu)	축구
taekwondo	*taekwondo* (tay-kwahn-doh)	태권도
tennis	*tenisu* (tay-nee-suu)	테니스
volleyball	*yoga* (yoh-gah)	요가

Do you like sports?

Undong choahaseyo? (Uhn-dong choh-ah-hah-say-yoh?) 운동 좋아하세요?

What sports do you play?

Musun undong haseyo? (Muu-suhn uhn-dong hah-say-yoh?) 무슨 운동 하세요?

What sports do you follow?

Otton undong-e kwanshimi issuseyo? (Oat-tone uhn-dong-eh kwahn-she-me ee-suu-say-yoh?) 어떤 운동에 관심이 있으세요?

Do you play golf?
Kolpu haljul aseyo? (Gohl-fuu hahl-juhl ah-say-yoh?) 골
프 할 줄 아세요?

Where do you play?
Odiso chiseyo? (Ah-dee-suh chee-say-yoh?) 어디서 치
세요?

How much are the green fees?
Yogum-i olma-e yo? (Yoh-guhm-ee ohl-mah-eh yoh?) 요
금이 얼마에요?

Do you play tennis?
Tenisu chiseyo? (Tay-nee-suu chee-say-yoh?) 테니스 치
세요?

Is the court public or private?
Kong-sol tenisu jangie yo, sa-sol tenisu jangie yo?
(Kohng-suhl tay-nee-suu jahng-ee-eh, sah-suhl tay-nee-
suu jahng-ee-eh yoh?) 공설 테니스장이에요, 사설테니
스 장이에요?

84 School *Hakkyo* (Hahk-k'yoh) 학교

student	*haksaeng* (hahk-sang) 학생
primary school	*chodeung hakkyo* (choh-dohng hahk-k'yoh) 초등 학교
high school	*kodeung hakkyo* (koh-duhng) 고등 학교
university	*taehakkyo* (tay-hahk-k'yoh) 대학교
graduate student	*tae hagwonsaeng* (tay hah-gwon-sang) 대학원생
private school	*sarip hakkyo* (sah-reep hahk-k'yoh) 사립 학교

Are you still a student?
Ajigdo haksaeng imnikka? (Ah-jeeg-doh hahk-sang eem-
nee-kah?) 아직도 학생 입니까?

What university do you attend?

Onu taeha-ge tanishimnikka? (Oh-nuu tay-hah-geh tah-nee-sheem-nee-kah?) 어느 대학에 다니십니까?

Are you a student at Seoul National University?

Chodurun Soul taehakkyo haksaengdur imnikka? (Chuh-duh-ruun Sole tay-hahk-k'yoh hahk-sang-duhr eem-nee-kah?) 저들은 서울대학교 학생들입니까?

What are you studying?

Musun kongbu-rul haseyo? (Muu-suhn kong-buu-ruhl hah-say-yoh?) 무슨 공부를 하세요?

What university did you graduate from?

Onu taeha-gul choropaessumnikka? (Oh-nuu tay-hah-guhl choh-rope-pay-sume-nee-kah?) 어느 대학을 졸업했습니까?

85 Birthday *Saengil* (Sang-eel) 생일

When is your birthday?

Saeng-iri onje eyo? (Sang-ee-ree uhn-jeh eh-yoh?) 생일이 언제예요?

My birthday is next week.

Nae saengil-i taum chu-e issumnida (Nay sang-eel-ee taj-uhm chuu-eh ees-sume-nee-dah) 내 생일이 다음 주에 있습니다.

Congratulations!

Chukahaeyo! (Chuu-kah-hay-yoh!) 축하해요!

Happy birthday!

Saeng-il chukka haeyo! (Sang-eel chuuk-kah hay-yoh!) 생일 축하해요!

My birthday is on _____ .

Che saeng-irun _____ (Cheh sang-ee-ruhn _____) 제 생일은 _____

Would you like to come to my party?
Nae patie oshiji ankessumnikka? (Nay pah-tee oh-she-jee ahn-keh-sume-nee-kah?) 내 파티에 오시지 않겠습니까?

Thank you for the present.
Sonmul kamsahamnida (Suhn-muhl kahm-sah-hahm-nee-dah) 선물 감사합니다.

86 Anniversary *Kinyomil* (Keen-yuh-meel) 기념일

wedding anniversary	*kyorhon kinyomil* (k'yuhr-hone keen-yuh-meel) 결혼 기념일

Today is our anniversary.
Onu-run chohi-dul-ui kinyomil imnida (Oh-nuu-ruhn choh-he-duhl-we keen-yoh-meel eem-nee-dah) 오늘은 저희들의 기념일입니다.

87 Movies *Yonghwa* (Yuhng-hwah) 영화

What movie is playing?
Yonghwa gwaneso mwol sangyong haeyo? (Yuhng-hwah gwahn-eh suh mwahl sahng-yuhng hay-yoh?) 영화관에서 뭘 상영해요?

Does it have English subtitles?
Yong-O chamak nawayo? (Yuhng-Oh chah-mahk nah-wah-yoh?) 영어 자막나와요?

88 Date (romantic) *Teitu* (Day-tuu) 데이트

café	*kape* (kah-peh) 카페
traditional teahouse	*chongtong chatchibe* (chohng-tohng chah-chee-beh) 전통 찻집
nightclub	*naitu* (nigh-tuu) 나이트
karaoke bar "singing rooms"	*norae bang* (No-ray bahng) 노래방

theater *kukchang* (Kuhk-chahng) 극장

What are you doing this evening?
Onul bame mwo haseyo? (Oh-nuhl bah-meh mwah hah-say-yoh?) 오늘밤에 뭐하세요?

How about going out for a drink?
Sul mashiro kalkkayo? (Suhl mah-she-ruh kahl-kah-yoh?)
술 마시러 갈까요?

Let's go dancing.
Chumchugo shipoyo (Chuum-chuugo ship-uh-yoh)
춤추고 싶어요.

Where shall we meet?
Odiso mannalkkayo? (Ah-dee-suh mahn-nahl-kah-yoh?)
어디서 만날까요?

What time shall we meet?
Myoshie mannalkkayo? (M'yuh-she-eh mahn-nahl-kah-you?) 몇시에 만날까요?

Would you like to dance?
Chum chushillaeyo? (Chuum chuu-sheel-lay-yoh?)
춤 추실래요?

What kind of music do you like?
Otton umagul choa haseyo? (Oat-ton uh-mah-guhl choh-ah hah-say-yoh?) 어떤 음악을 좋아 하세요?

We have a date tomorrow.
Naeil mannal teitu issuminda (Nay-ell mahn-nahl day-tuu ee-sume-nee-dah) 내일 만날 데이트 있습니다.

May I telephone you?
Chonhwa haedo dwaeyo? (Chone-hwah hay-doh dway-yoh?) 전화해도 돼요?

89 Wedding *Kyoron* (K'yuh-rone) 결혼

engagement	*yakon* (yah-kone) 약혼
bride	*shinbu* (sheen-buu) 신부
groom	*shillang* (sheel-lahng) 신랑
wedding cake	*weding keiku* (weh-deeng kay-kuu) 웨딩 케이크
wedding present	*weding sonmul* (weh-deeng suhn-muhl) 웨딩 선물
honeymoon	*shinhon yohaeng* (sheen-hone yuh-hang) 신혼 여행

90 Business *Bijinesu* (Bee-jee-nay-suu) 비즈니스

businessperson	*shiropka* (she-rup-kah) 실업가; *sangin* (sahng-een) 상인
business hours	*yongop shigan* (yuhng-gup she-gahn) 영업시간
business drink	*kyojesul* (k'yoh-jay-suhl)* 교제 술

*Drinking sessions play a significant role in business relationships in Korea. For a detailed explanation, refer to *Korean Business Etiquette* (Tuttle Publishing Group)

occupation	*chigop* (chee-gup) 직업

What is your business?
Chigobi muoshimnikka? (Chee-guh-bee mwah-sheem-nee-kah?) 직업이 무엇입니까?

91 Agent (business) *Tairiin* (Die-ree-een) 대리인

real estate agent	*poktok pang* (poke-toke pahng) 복덕방

I have an agent in Seoul.
Soul-e tairiin issumnida (Sohl-eh dai-ree-een ee-sume-nee-dah) 서울에 대리인이 있습니다

Do you have an agent in Pusan?

Busan-e tairiin issumnikka? (Buu-sahn-eh die-ree-een ee-sume-nee-kah?) 부산에 대리인이 있습니까?

Would you please recommend a good real estate agent?

Choun poktok pang-rul sogaehae chushiji ankessumi-nikka? (Choh-uhn poke-toke pahng-ruhl so-gay-hay chuu-she-jii ahn-keh-sume-nee-kah?) 좋은 복덕방을 소개해 주시지않겠습니까?

92 Agreement / Contract *Kyeyak* (Kay-yahk) 계약

house rental agreement

kaok imdae kyeyak (kah-oak eem-dy kay-yahk) 가옥임대계약

cancel a contract

kyeyag-ul haejehada (kay-yahg-uhl hay-jeh-hah-dah) 계약을 해제하다

We must have a contract.

Urinum kyeyak haeyahapnida (Uu-ree-nuhm kay-yahk hay-yah-hahp-nee-dah) 우리는 계약해야합니다.

Please sign this contract.

I kyehak-e somyong hashipshio (Ee kay-yahk-eh sah-m'yung hah-ship-she-oh) 이 계약에 서명하십시오.

I want to cancel this contract.

Kyeyak-ul chwisohago shipsumnida (Kay-yahk-uhl chwee-so-hah-go ship-sume-nee-dah) 계약을 취소하고 싶습니다.

Where do I sign?

Ssain-eul odie hajiyo? (Sign-ruhl ah-dee-eh hah-jee-yoh?) 싸인을 어디에 하지요?

93 Appointment *Yaksok* (yahk-soak) 약속

Are you busy now?
Chigum pappu shimnikka? (Chee-guhm pah-puh sheem-nee-kah?) 지금 바쁘십니까?

I have an appointment.
Yaksog-i issumnida (Yahk-soag-ee ee-sume-nee-dah) 약속이 있습니다.

How much do you charge for a consultation?
Uinon lyonun irhoe-e olma imnikka? (We-non-leo-nuun er-hway-e ohlm-mah eem-nee-kah?) 의논료는 일 회에 얼마입니까?

Are there many attorneys in Korea?
Hanguk-e nun pyonhosa duli manssumnikka? (Hah-guuk-eh nuun pyahn-hoh-sah duh-lee mahn-sume-nee-kah?) 한국에는 변호사들이 많습니까?

94 Bank* *Unhaeng* (Uhn-hang) 은행

ATM *Hyon Gumji Gupki* (Hyun Guhm-jee Guhp-kee) 현금지급기

*Banking in Korea is highly automated.

I need to go to a bank.
Unhaeng-e kaya hamnida (Uhn-hang-eh kah-yah hahm-nee-dah) 은행에 가야합니다.

What time do banks open?
Unhaeng-un myot shie yomnikka? (Uhn-hang-uhn m'yuht-she-eh yahm-nee-kah?) 은행은 몇시에 엽니까?

Please change these dollars into Korean currency.
I ttal-lo-rul won-eu-ru chom pakkwo chuseyo (Ee dal-lah-ruhl won-yu-ruu chome pahk-way chuu-say-you) 이 달러를 원으로 좀 바꿔주세요.

79

95 Border (of country) *Kukggyong* (Kuke-kyahng) 국경

How far is the border from here?
Yogi-so kukggyong kkaji olmana momnikka? (Yah-ghee-sah kuke-kyahng kah-jee ahl-mah-nah mahm-nee-kah?) 여기서 국경까지 얼마나 멉니까?

96 Born *Taeonan* (Tay-uh-nahn) 태어난

What year were you born?
Tangshin-un myon-nyou-e taeona sumnika? (Tahng-sheen-uhn m'yohn-n'yoh-eh tay-uh-nah sume-nee-kah?) 당신은 몇년에 태어났습니까?

Where were you born?
Odiso taeona sumnikka? (Ah-dee-suh tay-uh-nah sume-nee-kah?) 어디서 태어났습니까?

97 Citizen *Shimin* (She-meen) 시민

Where are you from?
Odi-e seo o-shyeo sseo yo? (Ah-dee-eh oh-shay say-oh yoh?) 어디에서 오셨어요?

Are you a Korean citizen?
Tangshin-un Hanguk shimin imnikka? (Tahng-sheen-uhn Hahn-guuk she-meen eem-nee-kah?) 당신은 한국시민 입니까?

Where were you born?
Kohyang-i odiseyo? (Koh-hyahng-ee ah-dee-say-yoh?) 고향이 어디세요?

Where do you live?
Odi saseyo? (Ah-dee sah-say-yoh?) 어디 사세요?

I'm American.
Chonun Miguksaram-i e yo (Choh-nuun Me-guuk-sah-rahm-ee eh-yoh) 저는 미국 사람이에요.

Australian	*Hojusaram* (Hoh-juu-sah-rahm) 호주사람
Canadian	*Kanadasaram* (Kaeh-nah-dah-sah-rahm) 캐나다사람
British	*Yongguksaram* (Yohng-guuk-sah-rahm) 영국 사람

98 Country *Nara* (Nah-rah) 나라

What country are you from?
Onu nara chulshin imnika? (Oh-nuu nah-rah chuul-sheen eem-nee-kah?) 어느 나라 출신입니까?

Is Korea your native country?
Hanguk-un tangshin-e kohyang imnikka? (Hahn-guuk-uhn tahng-sheen-eh koh-yahng eem-ne-kah?) 한국은 당신의 고향입니까?

99 Consulate *Yongsagwan* (Yahng-sahg-wahn) 영사관

Is there an American consulate here?
Yogi-e Migug-ui yongsagwan-i issumika? (Yah-ghee-eh Me-guug-we yahng-sahg-wahn-ee ee-sume-nee-kah?) 여기에 미국 영사관이 있습니까?

Embassy *Taesagwan* (Tay-sah-gwahn) 대사관

Please take me to the American Embassy.
Meigug Taesagwan-e kkaji kapshida (May-guug Tay-sah-gwahn-eh kah-jee kahp-she-dah) 미국대사관에 같이 갑시다.

100 Home / House *Chip* (Cheep) 집

household (family)	*kajong* (kah-johng) 가정
kitchen	*chubang* (chuu-bahng) 주방
living (setting) room	*koshil* (kuu-sheel) 거실
dining room	*shi tang* (she tahng) 식당
dinner	*chongchan* (chuung-chahn) 정찬
dinner party	*man chanhoe* (mahn chahn-whay) 만찬회
bathroom	*yokshil* (yoke-sheel) 욕실

Thank you for the invitation.

Chodaehae chusyoso kamsahamnida (Choh-day-hay chuu-show-suh kahm-sah-hahm-nee-dah) 초대해 주셔서 감사합니다.

This looks delicious!

Chal mokke ssumnida* (Chahl moke-kuh sume-nee-dah) 잘 먹겠습니다.

*Literally, "I will eat well," said by the guest at the beginning of a meal.

Thank you for a wonderful meal.

Hullyunghan shiksa kamsa hamnida (Huhl-yuhng-hahn sheek-sah kahm-sah hahm-nee-dah) 훌륭한 식사 삼사합니다.

Thank you for the delicious food.

Chal mogosseoyo (Chahl moh-guh-suh-yoh) 잘 먹었어요.

I enjoyed it very much.

Maeu maditke mogossumnida (My-uu mah-dee-kuh moh-guh-sume-nee-dah) 매우 맛있게 먹었습니다.

Goodbye!

Annyonghi kyeseyo (Ahn-n'yohng-he keh-say-yoh) 안녕히 계세요.

PART 2

General Information

Measurements

measurements *Chisu* (chee-suu) 치수

Please take my measurements.
Chisu-rul chae chuseyo (Chee-suu-ruhl chay chuu-say-yoh)
치수를 재주세요.

1 *sentimito* (sen-tee-mee-tah) 센티미터
  = 0.3987 *inchi* (in-chee) 인치
30.40 *sentimito* (sen-tee-mee-tah) 센티미터
  = 1 *puteu* (pu-tuh) 인치
1 *mito* (mee-tah) 미터 = 3.281 *piteu* (pee-tuh) 피트
1 *killomito* (keel-loh-mee-tah) 킬로머터
  = 0.6214 *mail* (mah-eel) 마일

1 *geuraem* (guh-rahm) 그램 = 0.03527 *ounseu* (oun-suh) 온스
1 *killogeuraem* (Keel-loh-guh-rahm) 킬로그램
  = 2.205 *paundeu* (poun-duh) 파운드
1 *ounseu* (oun-suh) 온스 = 28.35 *geuraem* (guh-rahm) 그램
1 *paundeu* (poun-duh) 파운드
  = 453.6 *geuraem* (guh-rahm) 그램

Personal Titles

The Korean language has many traditional forms of address for individuals, depending on their gender, age, social class, relationship and so on. Learning and using them correctly is a major chore. As a result, more and more Koreans are resorting to the use of the common English titles even when dealing with other Koreans. The use of English titles by foreigners is perfectly acceptable.

Miss	*Misu* (mee-suu) 미스; *Yang* (yahng) 양
Mr.	*Misuto* (miss-tah) 미스터; *Ssi* (sshe) 씨
also:	
	Songsangnim (suung-sang-neem) 선생님
Mrs.	*Misesu* (Me-say-suu) 미세스;
	chubu (chuu-buu) 주부

Academic Titles

dean	*hakchang* (hahk-chahng) 학장
lecturer	*kangsa* (kahng-sah) 강사
full-time lecturer	*chonim kangsa* (chuh-neem kahng-sah) 전임강사
professor	*kyosu* (k'yoe-suu) 교수
scholar	*hakcha* (hahk-chah) 학자
teacher	*kyosa* (k'yoe-sah) 교사

Business & Professional Titles

ambassador	*taesa* (day-sah) 대사
architect	*konchukkisa* (kuh-ahn-chuke-ke-sah) 건축기사
artist	*yesulga* (yay-suhl-gah) 예술가
athlete	*undongson-su* (unn-doong-sun-suu) 운동선수
businessman	*saopka* (sah-up-kah) 사업가
dentist	*chikkwaeuisa* (cheek-kway-we-sah) 치과의사

diplomat	*oegyogwan* (way-g'yoh-gwahn) 외교관
doctor	*euisa* (eh-wee-sah) 의사
engineer	*kisuljja* (kee-suhl-jah) 기술자
company executive	*hoesa kanbu* (whay-sah kahn-buu) 회사 간부
government official	*kwalli* (kwahl-lee) 관리
homemaker	*kajongjubu* (kah-jung-juu-buu) 가정주부
lawyer	*pyonhosa* (p'yone-hoh-sah) 변호사
manager	*chibaein* (chee-bay-een) 지배인
military officer	*yukkun changgyo* (yuke-kuun chahng-g'yoe) 육군장교
nurse	*kanhowon* (kahn-hoh-wan) 간호원
office worker	*sa muwon* (sah muu-wan) 사무원
politician	*chongchiga* (chohng-chee-gah) 정치가
private secretary	*pisu* (bee-suu) 비서
scientist	*kwahakcha* (kwah-hahk-chah) 과학자
soldier	*kunin* (kuun-een) 군인
journalist	*shinmun chapchi kija* (sheen-muun chahp-chee kee-jah) 신문 잡지 기자
author	*choja* (chu-jah) 저자
novelist/writer	*chakka* (chack-kah) 작가

Holidays

national holiday	*kukkyongil* (kuuk-k'yohng-eel) 국경일
vacation	*hyuil* (h'yuu-eel) 휴일
New Year's Day (January 1)	*Shin-jong Sol-lal)* (Sheen-johng sohl-lahl) 신정 설날
Independence Day (March 1)	*Sam-il Jol* (Sahn-eel Johl) 삼일절

Arbor Day (April 5)	*Shing-mo Gil* (Sheeng-moh Geel) 식목일
Children's Day (May 5)	*Eorin-e Nal* (Eh-yoh-reen-ee Nahl) 어린이날
Memorial Day (June 6)	*Hyon-chung Il* (H'yohn-chung Eel) 현충일
Constitution Day (July 17)	*Che-hon Jeol* (Chuh-hohn Johl) 제헌절
Liberation Day (August 15)	*Kwang-bok Jol* (Kwahng-boak Johl) 광복절
Thanksgiving Day (8th lunar month, 15th day)	*Chusok* (Chuu-soak) 추석
Armed Forces Day (October 1)	*Kukukkun-eul Nal* (Kuu-kuu-kkuun-yuhl Nahl) 국군의 날
National Foundation Day (October 3)	*Kae Chon Jol* (Kay Chohn Johl) 개천절
Hangul Day (October 9)	*Hangul Lal* (Hahn-guhl Lahl) 한글날
Christmas Day (December 25)	*Song-tahn Jol* (Sahng-tahn Johl) 성탄절

Popular Destinations in Seoul

American Embassy	*Miguk Taesagwan* (Me-guukTay-sah-gwahn) 미국 대사관
Chinese Embassy	*Chungguk-ui Taesagwan* (Chuung-guuk-we Tay-sah-gwahn) 중국 대사관
Japanese Embassy	*Ilbon-ui Taesagwan* (Eel-bohn-we Tay-sah-gwahn) 일본 대사관
East Gate	*Tong Daemun* (Toong Day-muun) 동대문

Itaewon Shopping District	*Itaewon Syoping Kuyok* (Ee-tay-won Shope-peeng Kuh-yuk) 이태원 쇼핑 구역
Great South Gate Market	*Nam Dae Mun Shijang* (Nahm Day Muun She-jahng) 남대문 시장
Kyongbok Palace	*Kyongbok Kung* (K'yohng-bok Kuung) 경복궁
National Central Museum [on Kyongbok Palace grounds]	*Kungnip Chungang Pangmulgwan* (Kuung-neep Chuun-gahng Pahng-muhl Gwahn) 국립중앙 박물관
National Folklore Museum	*Minsok Pangmul Gwan* (Meen-soak Pahng-muhl-gwahn) 민속 박물관
Panmunjom/DMZ	*Panmunjom* (Pahn-muun-johm) 판문점
Pulguk Temple	*Pulguk Sa* (Puhl-guuk Sah) 불국사
Secret Garden	*Pi Won* (Bee Won) 비원
Seoul Arts Center	*Yesure Chong Dang* (Yay-suu-ray Chong Dahng) 예술의 전당
South Mountain Park	*Nam San Kongwon* (Nahm Sahn Kong-wohn) 남산 공원
South Mountain Tower	*Nam San Tawo* (Nahm Sahn Tao-ah) 남산 타워
Toksu Palace	*Tokusu Gung* (Tuhk-suu Guung) 덕수궁

PART 3

Pronunciation Guide
For Key Names & Signs

The Nine Provinces

Chejudo (Cheh-juu-doh) 제주도
Chollabuk-do (Chol-la-buuk-doh) 전라북도
Chollanam-do (Chol-la-nahm-doh) 전라남도
Ch'ungch'ongbuk-do (Chuung-chohng-buuk-doh) 충청북도
Ch'ungch'ongnam-do (Chuung-chohng-nahm-doh) 충청남도
Kangwon-do (Kahng-won-doh) 강원도
Kyonggi-do (K'yohng-ghee-doh) 경기도
Kyongsangbuk-do (K'yohng-sahng-buuk-doh) 경상북도
Kyongsangnam-do (K'yohng-sahn-nahm-doe) 경상남도

Major Cities

Seoul (So-uhl) 서울
Pusan (Buu-sahn) 부산
Taegu (Tay-guu) 대구
Inch'on (Inn-chahn) 인천
Kwangju (Kwahng-juu) 광주
Taejon (Tay-joan) 대전
Kyongju (K'yohng-juu) 경주
Pohang (Poe-hahng) 포항
Chunchon (Chune-chahn) 춘천

Other Key Words

capital	*sudo* (suu-doh)	수도
city	*toshi* (toh-she)	도시
town	*sodoshi* (soh-doe-she)	소도시
village	*maeul* (may-uhl)	마을
hill	*ondok* (ahn-doak)	언덕
mountain	*san* (sahn)	산
lake	*hosu* (hoh-suu)	호수
coast	*haean* (hay-ahn)	해안
ocean	*pada* (pah-dah)	바다
Pacific Ocean	*Tae-p'yong Yang* (Day P'-yohng Yahng)	태평양
East Sea	*Tong Hae* (Doong Hay)	동해
Yellow Sea	*Hwang Hae* (Hwahng Hay)	황해
province	*to / do* (doh)	도
river	*kang* (kahng)	강
rural area	*shi gol* (she guhl)	시골

Common Signs

Knowing how to read public signs is one of the most important language assets one can have when visiting a foreign country. Here are some of the important signs you will see in Korea:

Entrance	*Ipku* (Eep-kuu)	입구
Push	*Milda* (Meel-dah)	밀다
Pull	*Dang-gi-da* (Tah-gah-chee)	당기다
Exit	*Chulgu* (Chul-guu)	출구
Emergency Exit	*Pisang Gu* (Bee-sahng Guu)	비상구
Toilet	*Pyongi* (Bee-yohn-ghee)	변기
Men	*Namja* (Nahm-jah)	남자
Women	*Yoja* (Yoh-jah)	여자
Open	*Yolda* (Yohl-dah)	열다

Closed	*Tatta* (Daht-tah) 닫다
Danger	*Wihom* (Wee-huum) 위험
No Smoking	*Kum Yon* (Kuum Yohn) 금연
Fire Alarm	*Hwajae Kyongbogi* (Hwah-jay K'yohng-boh-ghee) 화재 경보기
Fire Extinguisher	*Hwajae Sohwagi* (Hwah-jay Soh-whah-ghee) 화재 소화기
Information	*Annae So* (Ahn-nay Soh) 안내소
Cashier	*Chulnapkye* (Chul-nop-kay) 출납계
Parking Lot	*Chucha Jang* (Chuu-chah Jahng) 주차장
Hospital	*Pyongwon* (B'yohng-won) 병원

PART 4

Additional Vocabulary

[A]

abroad (overseas)	*haeoe-e* (hay-way-eh)	해외에
accessory	*pusokpum* (puu-soh-kuum)	부속품
accident	*sago* (sah-goh)	사고
accommoda-tion (lodging)	*suksso* (suuk-soh)	숙소
account	*kyesan* (kay-sahn)	계산
accountant	*hoegyesa* (whey-gay-sah)	회계사
acquaintance	*anun saram* (ah-nun sah-rahm)	아는 사람
actor	*paeu* (pay-uu)	배우
acupuncture	*chimchiryo* (cheem-chee-rio)	침치료
address (location)	*chuso* (chuu-soh)	주소
address (speech)	*yonsol* (yohn-sohl)	연설
admission	*ipchang* (eep-chahng)	입장
admission fee	*ipchang nyo* (eep-chahng n'yoh)	입장료
admission ticket	*ipchang kwon* (eep-chahng kwun)	입장권
advertise	*kwanggohada* (kwahng-goh-hah-dah)	광고하다
advertisement	*kwanggo* (kwahng-goh)	광고
help wanted ad	*kuin kwanggo* (kuu-een kwahng-goh)	구인 광고
job wanted ad	*kujik kwanggo* (kuu-jeek kwahng-goh)	구직광고

91

advice	*chunggo* (chuung-goh)	충고
adviser	*choonja* (choh-unn-jah)	조언자
affair (romantic)	*wa param-ul piuda* (wah pah-ram-uhl pee-uu-dah)	바람을 피우다
agent	*taeri* (day-ree)	대리
agency	*taeri* (day-ree)	대리
agreement (assent)	*tongui* (dohng-we)	동의
agreement (contract)	*kyeyak* (kay-yahk)	계약
agriculture	*nongop* (nohn-guhp)	농업
AIDS	*EIJI* (a-e-jee)	에이즈
airbase	*konggun kiji* (kohng-guun kee-jee)	공군 기지
air force	*konggun* (kohng-guun)	공군
airport	*konghang* (kohng-hahng)	공항
aisle	*tong-no* (tuung-no)	통로
alarm clock	*allam shigye* (ah-lahm she-gay)	알람 시계
alcohol	*al-kol* (ah-kohl)	알콜
alien (foreigner)	*oegugin* (way-guug-een)	외국인
allergy	*allerugi* (ahl-lur-ghee)	알레르기
alley (back street)	*kolmok* (kohl-moak)	골목
alphabet	*alp'abet* (ahl-pah-bet)	알파벳
altitude	*kodo* (koh-doh)	고도
ambassador	*taesa* (tay-sah)	대사
ambulance	*ku-gup-cha* (kuu-guup-chah)	구급차
America	*Miguk* (Me-guuk)	미국
American	*Miguksaram* (Me-guuk-sah-rahm)	미국사람
American Embassy	*Miguk Taesagwan* (Me-guuk Tie-sah-gwahn)	미국 대사관
ancestor	*chosang* (choh-sahng)	조상
ancient	*kodaeui* (koh-day-we)	고대의

English	Romanization	Korean
animal	*tongmul* (tohng-muhl)	동물
anniversary	*kinyohmil* (keen-yuh-meel)	기념일
announcement	*kongpyo* (kohng-p'yoh)	공표
annual	*illyonui* (eel-lyuh-n'wee)	일년의
antibiotic	*hangsang mulchil* (hahng-sang muhl-cheel)	항생물질
antique	*koldongpum* (kohl-doong-puum)	골동품
antique shop	*koldongpum kage* (kohl-doong-puum kah-gay)	골동품 가게
apartment	*ap'atu* (ah-pah-tuh)	아파트
apologize	*sagwahada* (sahg-wah-hah-dah)	사과하다
apology	*sagwa* (sahg-wah)	사과
appendicitis	*maengjangyom* (mang-jahng-yum)	맹장염
appetite	*sigyok* (she-g'yoak)	식욕
appetizer	*an-ju* (ahn-juu)	안주
application	*chimang* (chee-mahng)	지망
appointment	*yaksok* (yahk-sohk)	약속
apprentice	*toje* (toh-jay)	도제
approval	*sungin* (suhn-geen)	승인
architecture	*konchuk* (kuhn-chuuk)	건축
army	*yukkun* (yuuk-kuun)	육군
arrival	*tochak* (toh-chock)	도착
arrival gate	*tochak mun* (toh-chock muun)	도착문
arrive	*tochakhada* (toh-chock-hah-dah)	도착하다
art gallery	*hwa rang* (hwah rahng)	화랑
artist	*yesulga* (yeh-suhl-gah)	예술가
Asia	*Asia* (Asia)	아시아
Asian	*Asia saram* (Asia sah-rahm)	아시아 사람
aspirin	*asupirin* (ahs-pee-reen)	아스피린
assistant	*chosu* (choh-suu)	조수

association	*hyopoe* (h'yoh-pway)	협회
athlete	*sonsu* (sohn-suu)	선수
athlete's foot	*mujom* (muu-joam)	무좀
Atlantic Ocean	*Taesoyang* (Day-suh-yahng)	대서양
atomic energy	*wonja ryok* (wahn-jah r'yuk)	원자력
attorney	*pyonhosa* (p'yuhn hoh-sah)	변호사
audience	*chongjung* (chohng-juhng)	청중
auditorium	*kangdang* (kahng-dahng)	강당
Australia	*hoju* (hoh-juu)	호주;
	Ostreillia (Australia)	오스트레일리아
author	*choja* (choh-jah)	저자
automobile	*chadongcha* (chah-dohng-chah)	자동차
autumn	*kaul* (kah-uhl)	가을
award	*sangpum* (sahng-pume)	상품

[B]

baby	*aegi* (aa-ghee)	애기
baby food	*yua shik* (yu-ah sheek)	유아식
baby sitter	*ai tolponun saram* (aye dohl-poh-nuhn sah-rahm)	아이 돌보는 사람
bachelor	*chonggak* (chohng-gahk)	총각
backpack	*paenang* (pay-nahng)	배낭 .
badge	*paeji* (bay-jee)	배지
bag	*kabang* (kah-bahng)	가방
baggage	*chim* (cheem)	짐
baggage claim	*suha mul* (suu-hah muhl)	수하물
bakery	*pangjip* (pahng-jeep)	빵집
banana	*banana* (bah-nah-nah)	바나나
bandage	*pungdae* (puung-day)	붕대
band-aid	*ilhoyongpanchang-go* (eel-hoh-yohng-pahn-chahng-go)	일회용 반창고
bank	*unhang* (uun-hang)	은행
banker	*unhangga* (uun-hang-gah)	은행가

banquet	*yonhoe* (yuun-whey)	연회
bar	*ppa* (bah)	바
barber	*ibalssa* (ee-bahl-sah)	이발사
barbershop	*ibalso* (ee-bahl-suh)	이발소
bargain	*hungjong* (hung-juung)	흥정
barley tea	*poricha* (pah-ree-chah)	보리차
barter	*mulmul kyohwan* (muhl-muhl k'yoh-won)	물물 교환
baseball	*yagu* (yah-guu)	야구
basketball	*nonggu* (nohng-guu)	농구
bath	*mogyok* (moag-yoak)	목욕
bath house	*mogyok tang* (moag-yoak tahng)	목욕탕
bathing suit	*suyong bok* (suu-yuhng bohk)	수영복
bathroom	*mogyokssil* (moag-yoak-sheel)	목욕실
bathtub	*mogyok tong* (moag-yoak tahng)	목욕통
batteries	*boetori* (baa-toh-ree)	배터리
bay	*man* (mahn)	만
beach	*haesuyokjiang* (hay-suu-yoak-jee-ahng)	해수욕장
bean curd	*tu-bu* (tuh-buhh)	두부
beard	*suyom* (suu-yuhm)	수염
beautiful	*arumdaun* (ah-ruhm-dah-uun)	아름다운
beauty parlor	*mijang won* (me-jahng won)	미장원
bed	*chindae* (cheen-day)	침대
bedroom	*chimsil* (cheem-sheel)	침실
beef (broiled)	*pulgogi* (puhl-go-ghee)	불고기
beef ribs, broiled	*pulgalbi* (puhl-gahl-bee)	불갈비
beef steak	*pipusuteiku* (be-puu-stay-kuu)	비프스테이크

English	Romanization	Korean
beer	*maekchu* (make-chuu)	맥주
beer	*bio* (be-ah)	비어
beer hall	*bio hol* (be-ah hall)	비어홀
bellhop	*boi* (boy)	보이
bicycle	*chajongo* (chah-johng-oh)	자전거
bill	*kyesanso* (kay-sahn-suh)	계산소
bill(s), currency	*jari* (jah-ree)	짜리
birthday	*saengil* (sang-eel)	생일
birthday cake	*saengil keiku* (sang-ell kay-e-kuu)	생일 케이크
black market	*amshijang* (ahm-she-jahng)	암시장
blanket	*tamnyo* (dahm-n'yoh)	담요
blond	*kumbarui* (kuhm-bahr-we)	금발의
blood	*pi* (bee)	피
blood pressure	*hyo rap* (h'yuh rahp)	혈압
boat	*pae* (pay)	배
bomb	*poktan* (poak-than)	폭탄
bone	*pyo* (p'yoh)	뼈
bonus	*ponosu* (boh-nah-suu)	보너스
book	*chaek* (chake)	책
bookstore	*sojom* (suh-juum)	서점
booth (stand)	*pusu* (buu-suu)	부스
border	*kukkyong* (kuuk-k'yung)	국경
bosom	*kasum* (kah-suhm)	가슴
boss	*bosu* (boh-suu)	보스
bottle	*pyong* (b'yohng)	병
bouquet	*kkottabal* (koht-tah-bahl)	꽃다발
bowl	*sabal* (sah-bahl)	사발
box	*sangja* (sahng-jah)	상자
box lunch (Korean)	*toshirak* (toh-she-rahk)	도시락
boy friend	*boi furendu* (boy fu-ren-duu)	보이 프렌드
branch (office)	*chijom* (chee-juum)	지점
brand	*sangpyo* (sahng-p'yoh)	상표
bread	*pang* (pahng)	빵

breakfast	*achimshiksa* (ah-cheem-sheek-sah)	아침식사
	choban (choh-bahn)	조반
brewery	*yangjojang* (yahng-joh-jahng)	양조장
bribe	*noemul* (no-eh-muhl)	뇌물
bride	*shinbu* (sheen-buu)	신부
bridegroom	*shillang* (sheel-lahng)	신랑
briefcase	*kabang* (kah-bahng)	가방
Britain	*Yongguk* (Yohng-guuk)	영국
British (person)	*Yongguksaram* (Yohng-guuk-sah-rahm)	영국사람
British Embassy	*Yongguk Taesagwan* (Yohng-guuk Tay-sah-gwahn)	영국대사관
brochure	*sochaekcha* (soh-chake-chah)	소책자
broker	*purouko* (buu-roh-kah)	브로커
brothel	*yugwak* (yuug-wahk)	유곽
Buddhism	*Pulgyo* (Puhl-g'yoh)	불교
Buddhist	*Pulgyodo* (Puhl-g'yoe-doh)	불교도
buddy (friend)	*chingu* (cheen-guu)	친구
budget	*yesan* (yay-sahn)	예산
buffet	*changchang* (chahng-chang)	부페
building	*bilding* (beel-deeng)	빌딩
burglar	*kangdo* (kahng-doe)	강도
bus	*bosu* (buh-suu)	버스
bus stop	*bosu chongnyujang* (buh-suu chong-n'yuu-jahng)	버스 정류장
business	*yongmu* (yohng-muu)	용무
business hours	*yongop shigan* (yohng-guup she-gahn)	영업시간
businessman	*shiropka* (she-rup-kah)	실업가
business occupation	*chigop* (chee-guhp)	직업
butter	*boto* (bah-tah)	버터

[C]

cab	*taekshi* (tack-she)	택시
cabaret	*kyabare* (k'yah-bah-ray)	캬바레
cable TV	*keibul tibi* (kay-e-buul-dee-bee)	케이블 티비
café	*kape* (kah-pay)	카페
cake	*keiku* (kay-e-kuu)	케이크
calculator	*kyesangi* (kay-sahn-ghee)	계산기
calendar	*tallyok* (tahl-l'yuhk)	달력
calligraphy	*sodo* (suh-doh)	서도
camera	*kamera* (kah-may-rah)	카메라
camera shop	*kamera kage* (kah-may-rah kah-gay)	카메라 가게
campus	*kaempous* (came-pah-suu)	캠퍼스
Canada	*Kanada* (Kaeh-nah-dah)	캐나다
Canadian	*Kanadasaram* (Kaeh-na-dah-sah-rahm)	캐나다사람
cancel	*malsarhada* (mahl-sahr-hah-dah)	말살하다
cancer	*am* (ahm)	암
cancer (breast)	*yubang-am* (yuu-bahng-ahm)	유방암
cancer (stomach)	*wiam* (we-ahm)	위암
candy	*kaendi* (candy)	캔디
capital (money)	*chabon* (chah-bohn)	자본
capitalism	*chabonjuui* (chah-bohn-juu-wee)	자본주의
capitalist	*chabonga* (chah-bohn-gah)	자본가
car	*cha* (chah)	차
card (business)	*myong ham* (m'yohng hahm)	명함
card (playing)	*turompu* (tuu-rahm-puu)	트럼프
carpenter	*moksu* (moke-suu)	목수
cash	*hyon-gum* (h'yuhn-guhm)	현금
cashier	*chulnapkye* (chul-nahp-keh)	출납계

catalog	*katallougu* (kah-tahl-low-guu)	카탈로그
centimeter	*sentimito* (sen-tee-mee-tah)	센티미터
ceremony	*yesik* (yay-sheek)	예식
chair	*uija* (we-jah)	의자
change (coins)	*chandon* (chahn-dohn)	잔돈
charge (price wanted)	*chaegim* (chay-geem)	책임
charity	*chabisim* (chah-bee-sheem)	자비심
charming	*maeryokchogin* (mayer-ryuk-chog-een)	매력적인
chauffeur	*unjonkisa* (uun-joan-kee-sah)	운전기사
check (bill)	*kyesanso* (kay-sahn-soh)	계산서
check (money)	*supyo* (suup-yoh)	수표
check-in (at airport)	*tapsung susok* (tahp-suung suu-soak)	탑승 수속
child	*ai* (aye)	아이
children	*aidul* (aye-duhl)	아이들
China	*Chunggong* (Chuung-gohng)	중국
Chinese language	*Chunggu-mal* (Chuung-guu mahl)	중국말
Chinese person	*Chungguk saram* (Chuung-guuk sah-rahm)	중국 사람
Chinese (thing)	*Chunggukui* (Chuung-guuk-we)	중국의
chocolate	*chokalet* (choh-kah-let)	쵸코렛
chopsticks	*chokkarak* (chuh-kah-rahk)	젓가락
church	*kyohoe* (k'yoh-whey)	교회
citizen	*shimin* (she-meen)	시민
citizenship	*shiminkwon* (she-meen-kwun)	시민권
claim	*yogu* (yoh-guu)	요구
climate	*kihu* (kee-huu)	기후
clock / watch	*shigye* (she-gay)	시계

coffee shop	*kopi shop* (koh-pee shop)	커피숍
coke	*kokakolla* (koh-kah-koh-lah)	코카콜라
comb	*moribit* (moh-ree-beet)	머리빗
common sense	*sangshik* (sahng-sheek)	상식
communism	*kongsanjuui* (kohng-sahn-juu-we)	공산주의
communist	*kongsanjuuija* (kohn-sahn-juu-we-jah)	공산주의자
compact disc	*kompaktu disuku* (kome-pahk-tuu-dees-kuu)	컴팩트 디스크
company	*hoesa* (hwey-sah)	회사
competitor	*kyongjengja* (k'yohng-jang-jah)	경쟁자
complaint	*pulpyong* (puhl-pyung)	불평
computer	*kompyuto* (kome-pyu-tah)	컴퓨터
concert	*umakoe* (uh-mah-koh-eh)	음악회
condoms	*kondom* (condom)	콘돔
conference	*hoeui* (hwey-we)	회의
confirmation	*hwaginso* (hwah-geen-soh)	확인서
Confucius	*Kongja* (Kohng-jah)	공자
consulate	*yongsagwan* (yuhng-sah-gwahn)	영사관
contact lens	*kontaktu renjo* (kohn-tack-tuu ren-ju)	콘텍트 렌즈
cookie	*kwaja* (kwah-jah)	과자
corn	*oksusu* (oak-suu-suu)	옥수수
courtyard	*tul* (duhl)	뜰
cover charge	*ipjiang nyo* (eep-jee-ahng n'yoh)	입장료
crab	*ke* (kay)	게
credit card	*kuridit kadu* (kuu-re-deet kah-duh)	크레디트 카드
cup	*kop* (kup)	컵
curfew	*tanghanggumji* (tohng-hahng guum-jee)	통행금지

currency (Korean)	*won* (won)	원
customer	*sonnim* (soan-neem)	손님
cute	*kwiyoun* (kwee-yuh-uun)	귀여운

[D]

daily	*maeil* (may-eel)	매일
damage	*sonhae* (sohn-hay)	손해
dangerous	*wihomhan* (we-huhm-hahn)	위험한
date (calendar)	*naljja* (nahl-jah)	날짜
date (romantic)	*teitu* (day-tuu)	데이트
date of birth	*saeng il* (sang eel)	생일
daughter	*dal* (dahl)	딸
decaffeinated coffee	*mukapein kopi* (muu-kah-pane koh-pee)	무카페인 커피
delicatessen	*shikpumjom* (sheek-pume-juhm)	식료품점
delivery	*paedal* (pay-dahl)	배달
democracy	*minjujui* (meen-juu-jwee)	민주주의
demonstration	*demo* (demo)	데모
department (in company)	*pu* (buu)	부
department store	*paek wajom* (pake wah-jum)	백화점
departure	*chubal* (chuu-bahl)	출발
design	*solgye* (suhl-geh)	설계
dessert	*husik* (huu-sheek)	후식
	tijotu (dee-jah-tuu)	디저트
destination	*mokchokchi* (moke-chuk-chee)	목적지
diabetes	*tangnyobyong* (tahng-n'yoh-byung)	당뇨병
dialect	*saturi* (sah-tuu-ree)	사투리
diapers (disposable)	*chongikijogwi* (chung-ee-kee-jog-we)	천 기저귀

101

diarrhea	*solsa* (suhl-sah)	설사
dictionary	*sojon* (soh-juhn)	사전
dining	*siksa* (sheek-sah)	식사
dining car	*sikttangcha* (sheek-dahng-chah)	식당차
dining room	*sikttang* (sheek-dahng)	식당
dinner	*chonyok* (chun-yuhk)	저녁
dirty	*toroun* (tuh-ruhn)	더러운
discount	*harin* (hah-reen)	할인
display (show)	*chonsihada* (chune-she-hah-dah)	전시하다
divorced	*ihonhan* (ee-hohn-hahn)	이혼한
DMZ (De-Militarized Zone)	*Pimujang Jidae* (Pee-muu-jahng Jee day)	비무장 지대
document	*munso* (muun-suh)	문서
door, gate	*mun* (muun)	문
downtown	*jungshimga* (jung-sheem-gah)	중심가
city center	*shinae* (she-nay)	시내
draft beer	*saeng maekchu* (sang make-juu)	생맥주
dress (Western)	*duresu* (du-res-suu)	드레스
dress (Korean)	*hanbok* (hahn-boak)	한복
driver	*unjonsu* (un-joan-sah)	운전수
driver's license	*unjon myonhojung* (uhn-joan m'yohn-hoh-juung)	운전 면허증
drugs	*mayak* (mah-yahk)	마약
drugstore	*yakkuk* (yahk-kuuk)	약국
drunk	*sulchwihan* (suhl-ch'we-hahn)	술취한
dry cleaning	*durai kulining* (duu-rye kuu-lee-neeng)	드라이 크리닝
duty	*uimu* (we-muu)	의무

[E]

ear	*kwi* (kwee)	귀
early	*irun* (ee-ruhn)	이른
early morning	*irun achim* (ee-ruhn ah-cheem)	이른 아침
earrings	*kwigori* (kwee-go-ree)	귀고리
earth	*chigu* (chee-guu)	지구
earthquake	*chijin* (chee-jeen)	지진
eat out	*oeshik hagi* (way-sheek hah-ghee)	외식 하기
economics	*kyongiehak* (k'yung-ee-eh-hahk)	경제학
economy	*kyongje* (k'yung-jay)	경제
education	*kyoyuk* (k'yoh-yuk)	교육
eggs	*kyeran* (kay-rahn)	계란
electrical appliance	*kajon chepum* (kah-joan cheh-puum)	가전 제품
electricity	*chongi* (chun-ghee)	전기
elevator	*ellibeiteo* (el-ee-bay-tor)	엘리베이터
embassy	*taesagwan* (tay-sah-gwahn)	대사관
emergency	*wigup* (we-guhp)	위급
emergency exit	*pisang gu* (pee-sahng guu)	비상구
employee	*pigoyong-in* (pee-go-yohng-een)	피고용인
employer	*koyongju* (koh-yohng-juu)	고용주
engagement	*yakon* (yah-kohn)	약혼
engagement ceremony	*yakon shik* (yah-kohn sheek)	약혼식
engine	*enjin* (in-jeen)	엔진
engineer	*kisuljia* (kee-suhl-jah)	기술자
England	*Yongguk* (Yohng-guuk)	영국
English language	*Yong o* (Yohng oh)	영어
entertainment (as in treat)	*chopttae* (chup-day)	접대

entrance	*iptchang* (eep-chahng)	입장
envelope	*pongfu* (pang-fuu)	봉투
escalator	*esukolleito* (es-ku-lay-tor)	에스컬레이터
etiquette	*etiket* (etiquette)	에티켓
Europe	*Yurop* (Yuu-ruhp)	유럽
European (person)	*Yuropsaram* (Yuu-ruhp-sah-ram)	유럽사람
evening	*pam* (bahm)	밤
everyday	*maeil* (may-eel)	매일
evidence	*chunggo* (chuhng-guh)	증거
examination (test)	*sihom* (she-huum)	시험
example	*ye* (yay)	예
exchange	*pakuda* (pahk-dah)	바꾸다
exchange rate	*hwan yul* (hwahn yuhl)	환율
executive	*hoesakanbu* (whey-sah-kahn-buu)	회사간부
exercise	*undong* (uhn-dong)	운동
exhibition	*chonshihoe* (chun-she-whey)	전시하다
exit	*chulgu* (chuhl-guu)	출구
expensive	*pissan* (bee-sahn)	비싼
export (v)	*suchulhada* (suu-chuhl-hah-dah)	수출하다
eye	*nun* (nuun)	눈

[F]

face	*eolgul* (ahl-guhl)	얼굴
factory	*kongjang* (kohn-jahng)	공장
fake	*katcha* (kaht-chah)	가짜
family	*kajok* (kah-joak)	가족
fan (hand held)	*puchae* (puu-chay)	부채
fan (electric)	*sonpunggi* (sahn-puhng-ghee)	선풍기
far	*molda* (mohl-dah)	멀다
fare	*yogum* (yoh-guum)	요금

farewell party	*songbyol hoe* (suung-b'yohl hoh-eh)	송별 회
farm	*nongga* (nohng-gah)	농가
favorite place (to shop, etc)	*tan gol* (than gohl)	단골
fax	*paeksu* (pake-suu)	팩스
fee	*yogum* (yoh-guum)	요금
female	*yoja* (yoh-jah)	여자
ferry	*peri* (bay-ree)	페리
ferryboat	*narutppae* (nah-ruut-pay)	나룻배
festival	*chukche* (chuuk-chuh)	축제
filling station	*chuyu so* (chuu-yuu soh)	주유소
film (camera)	*pillum* (pee-luum)	필름
fire (conflagration)	*hwajae* (hwah-jay)	화재
fireman	*hwabu* (hwah-buu)	화부
fireworks	*pulkkonnori* (puhl-kohn-no-ree)	불꽃놀이
first (in order)	*chot* (choat)	첫
first-aid kit	*kugup sangja* (kuu-guhp sahng-jah)	구급 상자
first-class seat	*il-dung sok* (eel-duhng suhk)	일등석
fish market	*susanmul shijang* (suu-sahn-muhl she-jahng)	수산물 시장
fixed price	*chong ga* (chohng gah)	정가
flag (national)	*kukki* (kuuk-kee)	국가
flashlight	*pullaeshi* (puhl-lie-she)	플래쉬
flight (air)	*pihaeng* (bee-hang)	비행
flood	*hongsu* (hohng-suu)	홍수
floor (of building)	*chung* (chuhng)	층
flower	*kot* (kaht)	꽃
flower shop	*kot jip* (kaht jeep)	꽃집
folk art	*minsok yesul* (meen-soak yay-suhl)	민속 예술

folk songs	*taejung gayo* (tay-juung gah-yoh)	대중 가요
food	*umshik* (uum-sheek)	음식
food (Korean)	*Hanshik* (Hahn-sheek)	한식
food (Western)	*Yangshik* (Yahng-sheek)	양식
food poisoning	*shik chungdok* (sheek chung-doak)	식중독
foot	*pal* (bahl)	발
football (American)	*Mishik chukku* (Me-sheek chuke-kuu)	미식축구
football (soccer)	*chuuku* (chuuk-kuu)	축구
foreigner	*woguksaram* (woh-guuk-sah-rahm)	외국사람
forest	*samnim* (sahm-neem)	삼림
fortune teller	*chomjaeng-i* (chohm-jang-ee)	점쟁이
France	*Purangsu* (Puu-rahng-suu)	프랑스
free (no charge)	*muryo* (muu-rio)	무료
free parking	*muryo chucha* (muu-rio chuu-chah)	무료 주차
friend	*chingu* (cheen-guu)	친구
friendship	*ujong* (uu-jung)	우정
fruit	*kwail* (kwah-eel)	과일
full	*kadukchan* (kah-duhk-chahn)	가득찬
funeral	*changnyeshik* (chahng-nay-sheek)	장례식
furnace	*hwaro* (whah-roh)	화로
furniture	*kagu* (kah-guu)	가구
future	*mirae* (me-ray)	미래

[G]

gamble	*tobak* (toh-bahk)	도박
game (event)	*kyonggi* (k'yohng-ghee)	경기
garage	*chago* (chah-go)	차고
garden	*chongwon* (chohng-won)	정원

garlic	*manul* (mah-nuhl)	마늘
gas	*gasu* (gah-suu)	가스
gasoline	*gasollin* (gah-so-leen)	가솔린
gas station	*chuyu so* (chuu-yuu soh)	주유소
gate	*mun* (muhn)	문
gentleman	*sinsa* (sheen-sah)	신사
German (person)	*Togilsaram* (Doh-geel-sah-ram)	독일사람
Germany	*Togil* (Doh-geel)	독일
gift	*sonmul* (sohn-muhl)	선물
gift shop	*sonmul kage* (sohn-muhl kah-gay)	선물 가게
ginseng	*insam* (en-sahm)	인삼
ginseng tea	*insam cha* (en-sahm chah)	인삼차
ginseng wine	*insam ju* (en-sahm juu)	인삼주
girl	*sonyo* (sohn-yuh)	소녀
girl friend	*yoja chingu* (yuh-jah cheen-guu)	여자친구
glasses (eye)	*angyong* (ahn-g'yohng)	안경
gloves	*changgap* (chahng-gahp)	장갑
gold	*kum* (kuhm)	금
golf	*kolpu* (gohl-puu)	골프
golf course	*kolpu kosu* (gohl-puu koh-suh)	골프 코스
government	*chongbu* (chohng-buu)	정부
governor	*chisa* (chee-sah)	지사
gram	*guraem* (gu-rahm)	그램
grandchild	*sonju* (sohn-juu)	손주
granddaughter	*sonnyo* (sohn-nyuh)	손녀
grandfather	*haraboji* (hah-rah-buh-jee)	할아버지
grandmother	*halmoni* (hahl-muh-nee)	할머니
groom	*shillang* (sheel-lahng)	신랑
guest	*sonnim* (sohn-neem)	손님
guide (person)	*kaidu* (guy-duu)	가이드
guidebook	*kaidubuk* (guy-duu buuk)	가이드북

gun	*chong* (chohng)	총
gym (health club)	*helsu jang* (hel-suu jahng)	헬스장
gymnasium	*chyukkwan* (chuck-kwahn)	체육관
gymnastics	*chejo* (cheh-joh)	체조

[H]

hair	*mori* (muh-ree)	머리
haircut	*heokotu* (hay-ah-kah-tuu)	헤어커트
hairdresser	*ibalssa* (ee-bahl-sah)	이발사
ham	*haem* (ham)	햄
handbag	*kabang* (kah-bahng)	가방
handicrafts	*sugongyepum* (suu-gohn-gay-puum)	수공예품
handmade	*sujepum* (suu-jay-puum)	수제품
harbor	*hanggu* (hahng-guu)	항구
hardware (computer)	*haduweo* (hah-duu-way-ah)	하드웨어
harvest	*chusu* (chuu-suu)	추수
hat	*moja* (moh-jah)	모자
head	*mori* (muh-ree)	머리
headache	*tutong* (duu-dohng)	두통
headquarters	*ponbu* (pohn-buu)	본부
health	*kongang* (kohn-gahng)	건강
hear	*turoyo* (tuh-ruh-yoh)	들어요
hearing aid	*pochonggi* (poh-chung-ghee)	보청기
heart	*shimjang* (sheem-jahng)	심장
heater	*hiteo* (he-tah)	히터
heavy	*mugoun* (muu-guh-unn)	무거운
highway	*kosoktoro* (koe-soak-doe-roe)	고속도로
hill	*ondok* (uhn-duk)	언덕
historical	*yoksaui* (yuk-sah-we)	역사의
history	*yoksa* (yuk-sah)	역사
hobby	*chwimi* (ch'we-me)	취미

hockey (ice)	*aisu haki* (aye-suu hah-kee)	아이스 하키
holiday	*hyuil* (h'yuu-eel)	휴일
(public	*kong hyuil* (kohng	공휴일
holiday)	h'yuu-eel)	
hometown	*kohyang* (koh-yahng)	고향
homosexual	*tongsong-ae-e* (tohng-suhng-aa-eh)	동성애
honey	*gul* (guhl)	꿀
honeymoon	*shinhon yohaeng* (sheen-hoan yuh-hang)	신혼 여행
Hong Kong	*Hong Kong* (Hong Kong)	홍콩
hospital	*pyongwon* (p'yohng-won)	병원
(private	*kaein pyongwon* (kay-een	개인병원
hospital)	p'yohng-won)	
hostess fee	*hosutesu tip* (hos-teh-suu teep)	호스테스 팁
(club)		
hot (to touch)	*dugoun* (duu-gah-uun)	뜨거운
hotel	*hot'el* (hotel)	호텔
hot springs	*on chon* (uhn juhn)	온천
hot weather	*toun* (tuh-uun)	더운
hour	*shigan* (she-gahn)	시간
house	*chip* (cheep)	집
housewife	*chubu* (chuu-buu)	주부
housework	*chibanil* (chee-bahn-eel)	집안일
humid	*supkiitta* (suup-keet-chan)	습기찬
hungry	*paegopuda* (pay-guh-puu-dah)	배고프다
hydrofoil	*sujungiksun* (su-jung-ik-suu)	수중익선

[I]

ice	*orum* (ah-ruum)	얼음
ice cream	*aisu kurim* (aye-suu kuu-reem)	아이스크림
ill (sick)	*apun* (ah-poon)	아픈
illegal	*pulppopui* (puhl-puhp-wee)	불법의

income	*suip* (suu-eep)	수입
industry	*sanop* (sah-nuhp)	산업
infant	*aegi* (aa-ghee)	애기
information desk	*annae so* (ahn-nay soh)	안내소
injection	*chusa* (chuu-sah)	주사
injury	*pusang* (puu-sahng)	부상
insurance	*pohom* (poh-hoam)	보험
interest (money)	*ija* (ee-jah)	이자
international	*kukchejogin* (kuuk-chay-jug-een)	국제적인
Internet café	*intonet kape* (in-tah-net kah-pay)	인터넷 카페
interpreter	*fongyokkwan* (fuung-yoke-kwahn)	번역관
intersection	*negori* (nay-guh-ree)	네거리
introduction	*sogae* (soh-gay)	소개
island	*som* (sohm)	섬
itinerary	*yojong* (yuh-johng)	여정
ivory	*sanga* (sahn-gah)	상아

[J]
jacket	*chaket* (chah-ket)	자켓
jade	*pichwi* (pee-chwee)	비취
Japan	*Ilbon* (Eel-bone)	일본
Japanese language	*Ilbon o* (Eel-bone oh)	일본어
Japanese (person)	*Ilbonsaram* (Eel-bone-sah-rahm)	일본사람
jazz	*jaju* (jah-juu)	재즈
jeans	*chongbaji* (chohng-bah-jee)	청바지
jewelry	*posok* (boh-suk)	보석
jewelry store	*posok sang* (boh-suk sahng)	보석상
job	*chigop* (chee-guhp)	직업

jogging	*choging* (jah-geen)	조깅
journalist	*kija* (kee-jah)	기자
journey	*yohaeng* (yu-hang)	여행
judo	*yudo* (yuu-doh)	유도
juice	*jusu* (juu-suu)	주스

[K]

karaoke	*noraebang* (noh-ray-bang)	노래방
karaoke bar	*karaoke ba* (kah-rah-oh-kay bah)	카라오케 바
karate	*karade* (kah-rah-day)	카라데
ketchup	*kechop* (keh-chup)	케챱
key	*yolso* (yohl-soh)	열쇠
kilogram	*killoguraem* (keel-loh-gu-rahm)	킬로그램
kilometer	*killomito* (keel-loh-me-tah)	킬로미터
kisaeng (female entertainer)	*kisaeng* (kee-sang)	기생
kiss	*kisu* (kee-suu)	키스
kitchen	*chubang* (chuu-bahng)	추방
knife	*naipu* (nie-puu)	나이프
Korea	*Hanguk* (Hahn-guuk)	한국
Korean (language)	*Hangug o* (Hahn-guug oh)	한국어
Korean (person)	*Hanguksaram* (Hahn-guuk-sah-rahm)	한국사람

[L]

lacquer ware	*najon chilgi* (nah-joan cheel-ghee)	나전 칠기
laundry (clothes)	*setangmul* (she-tahng-muhl)	세탁물
laundry (place)	*setakso* (say-tahk-soh)	세탁소
law	*pop* (puhp)	법
lawyer	*pyonhosa* (p'yohn-hoh-sah)	변호사

leather	*kajuk* (kah-juke)	가죽
lecture	*kangui* (kahng-we)	강의
leisure	*yoga* (yuh-gah)	여가
lemonade	*remoneidu* (remon-a-duu)	레모네이드
letter (written)	*pyonji* (p'yohn-jee)	편지
library	*tosogwan* (toh-suh-gwahn)	도서관
license	*hoga* (huh-gah)	허가
lifeguard	*inmyongkujowon* (een-m'yohng-kuu-joh-won)	인명구조원
light (electric)	*pul* (puhl)	불
lightbulb	*chongu* (chone-guu)	전구
liquor	*alkool umnyo* (alh-kah-ohl uum'nyoh)	알콜 음료
literature	*munhak* (muun-hhk)	문학
little (amount)	*chogum* (choh-guhm)	조금
little (size)	*chagum* (chah-guhm)	작은
loan	*taebu* (tay-buu)	대부
local bus	*maul bosu* (mahl bah-suu)	마을버스
lock	*chamulsoe* (chah-muhl-swey)	자물쇠
locker	*rok'o* (rah-kah)	락커
lost	*irun* (ee-ruhn)	잃은
lost-and-found office	*pun-shil-mul chwigup so* (puun-sheel-muhl chwee-guup soh)	분실물 취급소
lover	*aein* (aye-een)	애인
luck	*un* (uhn)	운
luggage	*chim* (cheem)	짐
luggage lockers	*chim pogwanso* (cheem pohg-wahn-soh)	짐 보관소
lumber	*chaemok* (chay-moak)	재목
lunch	*chomshim* (chum-sheem)	점심
lunch time	*chomshim shigan* (chum-sheem she-gahn)	점심시간
luxurious	*sachisuron* (sah-chee-suh-ruhn)	사치스런

luxury	*sachi* (sah-chee)	사치
[M]		
machine	*kigye* (kee-gay)	기계
made-in-country (Korea)	*kuksam pum* (kuuk-sahm pume)	국산품
maid	*hanyo* (hah-yoh)	하녀
magazine	*chapji* (chahp-jee)	잡지
magic	*masul* (mahl-suhl)	마술
mail	*pyonji* (p'yun-jee)	편지
mailbox	*uchetong* (uh-chay-tong)	우체통
manager	*chibaein* (chee-bay-een)	지배인
manager	*maenijo* (may-nee-jah)	매니저
Manchuria	*Manju* (Mahn-juu)	만주
map	*chido* (chee-duh)	지도
city map	*shinae chido* (she-nay jee-duh)	시내 지도
road map	*toro chido* (doh-roh jee-duh)	도로 지도
market (open air)	*shijang* (she-jahng)	시장
marriage	*kyolhon* (k'yohl-hoan)	결혼
married	*kyoron han* (k'yuh-rone hahn)	결혼한
martial arts	*musul* (muu-suhl)	무술
martial arts (Korean)	*taekkwondo* (tay-kwahn-doh)	태권도
massage	*anma* (ahn-mah)	안마
masseur/masseuse	*anmasa* (ahn-mah-sah)	안마사
math	*suhak* (suu-hahk)	수학
matinee	*natkongyon* (naht-kohng-yohn)	낮공연
measure	*chaeda* (chay-dah)	재다
mechanic	*chongbigong* (chong-bee-gohng)	정비공

medical insurance	*uiryobohom* (we-ruh-boh-hum)	의료보험
medicine	*yak* (yahk)	약
meeting	*hohap* (hwah-hahp)	회합
message	*meshiji* (may-she-jee)	메세지
Mexico	*Mekshiko* (Mek-she-koh)	멕시코
military	*kun* (kuun)	군
military service	*kunbong mu* (kuun-bohng-muu)	군복무
mineral water	*saengsu* (sang-suu)	생수
minister	*moksanim* (moke-sah-neem)	목사님
mirror	*koul* (koh-uul)	거울
missionary	*songyosa* (sahng-yoh-sah)	선교사
mistake	*shilsu* (sheel-suu)	실수
mobile phone	*haendu pon* (hane-duu pohn)	핸드폰
model (fashion)	*ponttuda* (pohn-duu-dah)	본뜨다
modern	*hyondaeui* (hyun-day-wee)	현대의
modern style	*sinsikui* (sheen-sheek-wee)	신식의
monk	*chung; sunim* (chuung; suh-neem)	중 ; 스님
mood, feelings	*kibun* (kee-boon)	기분
monsoon	*changma* (chahng-mah)	장마
mosque	*hogyosawon* (hoh-g'yoh-sah-won)	회교사원
mosquito	*mogi* (moh-ghee)	모기
mosquito coil	*mogi hyang* (moh-geeh h'yahng)	모기향
motel	*motel* (moh-tel)	모텔
mother	*omoni* (uh-muh-nee)	어머니
mother-in-law	*shiomoni* (she-uh-muh-nee)	시어머니
motorcycle	*otobai* (ah-toh-by)	오토바이
mountain	*san* (sahn)	산
movie	*yonghwa* (yohng-hwah)	영화
Mr., Mrs., Miss	*sshi* (sshe)	씨
murder	*sarin* (sah-reen)	살인

museum	*pangmulgwan* (pahng-muhl-wahn)	박물관
music	*umak* (uh-mahk)	음악
musical	*myujikal* (m'yuu-jee-kal)	뮤지컬
musician	*umakka* (uh-mahk-kah)	음악가

[N]

name	*irum* (ee-ruhm)	이름
napkin	*napkin* (nahp-keen)	냅킨
nation (state)	*kukka* (kuuk-kah)	국가
national	*kukka-e* (kuuk-kah-eh)	국가의
national holiday	*kukkyong il* (kuuk-k'yuhng eel)	국경일
nationality	*kukchok* (kuuk-chuk)	국적
national park	*kungnipkong won* (kuung-neep-kohng won)	국립공원
newspaper	*shinmun* (sheen-muun)	신문
newspaper (English)	*Yongjia shinmun* (Yohng-jah sheen-muun)	영자신문
night	*yagan* (yah-gahn)	야간
nightclub	*naitukullop* (nie-toh-kuu-lahb)	나이트클럽
noise	*soum* (soh-uhm)	소음
noisy	*shikkuroun* (sheek-kuh-roan)	시끄러운
noodles	*kuksu* (kuuk-suh)	국수
noon	*chong-o* (chung-oh)	정오
north	*puktchok* (puuk-choke)	북쪽
North Korea	*Pukan* (Puuk-ahn)	북한
novel	*sosol* (soh-suhl)	소설
nuclear	*wonjahangui* (wah-jah-hang-we)	원자핵의
number	*suryang* (suu-r'yahng)	수량
nurse	*kanhosa* (kahn-hoh-sah)	간호사

[O]

oatmeal	*otumil* (oh-toh-meel)	오트밀
occupation	*chigop* (chee-gahp)	직업
ocean	*taeyang* (tie-yahng)	태양
office	*samushil* (sah-muu-sheel)	사무실
office worker	*samu won* (sah-muu won)	사무원
official (gov't)	*kwanri* (kwahn-ree)	관리
oil (automobile)	*oil* (oh-eel)	오일
ointment	*yongo* (yuhn-go)	연고
open for business	*yong-opchung* (yuhng uhp-chung)	영업중
operator	*kyohwanwon* (k'yoh-hwahn-won)	교환원
opportunity	*kihoe* (kee-whey)	기회
optician	*angyongjom* (ahn-g'yohng-jome)	안경점
outline	*yungwak* (yuhn-gwahk)	윤곽
overcoat	*obokotu* (oh-bah-koh-tuu)	오버코트
oxygen	*san-so* (sahn-soh)	산소
oyster	*kul* (kuhl)	굴

[P]

pacemaker	*peisumeiko* (pay-suu-may-kah)	페이스메이커
Pacific Ocean	*Taepyong Yang* (Day-p'yuhng Yahng)	태평양
package	*chim* (cheem)	짐
pain	*kotong* (koh-dong)	고통
painful	*apun* (ah-poon)	아픈
palace	*wanggung* (wahng-guung)	왕궁
paper	*chongi* (chohng-ee)	종이
parcel	*sopo* (sope-oh)	소포
parents	*pumonim* (puu-moh-neem)	부모님
park	*kongwon* (kohng-won)	공원

parking lot	*chucha jang* (chuu-chah jahng)	주차장
party	*pati* (pah-tee)	파티
passenger	*sunggaek* (suhng-gake)	승객
passport	*yokwon* (yoh-kwahn)	여권
payment	*chibul* (chee-buhl)	지불
peanuts	*tangkong* (tahng-kohng)	땅콩
pearls	*chinju* (cheen-juu)	진주
pen	*pen* (pen)	펜
penicillin	*penishillin* (pen-e-sheel-leen)	페니실린
people	*saram-dul* (sah-rahm-duhl)	사람들
perfume	*hyangsu* (hyahng-suu)	향수
permission	*hoga* (huh-gah)	허가
pharmacy	*yakkuk* (yahk-kuuk)	약국
pickpocket	*somaechigi* (soh-may-chee-ghee)	소매치기
picture postcard	*kurim yopso* (kuu-reem yup-suh)	그림 엽서
pill	*allyak* (ahl-yahk)	알약
planet	*yusong* (yuu-suhng)	유성
platform (train)	*pullatpom* (plat-pome)	플랫폼
poetry	*si* (she)	시
police, officer	*kyongchal* (k'yung-chahl)	경찰
politician	*chongchiga* (chuhng-chee-gah)	정치가
politics	*chongchi* (chung-chee)	정치
popular music	*pap song* (pahp song)	팝송
population	*ingu* (een-guu)	인구
port	*hanggu* (hahng-guu)	항구
postcard	*upyonyopso* (uup-yohn-yup-suh)	우편엽서
post office	*ucheguk* (uu-chay-guuk)	우체국
potable water	*shik su* (sheek suu)	식수
pregnant (with child)	*imsinhan* (eem-sheen-hahn)	임신한

prescription	*chobang* (choh-bahng)	처방
president (of company)	*sajang* (sah-jahng)	사장
president (of nation)	*taetongnyong* (day-dohng-n'yohng)	대통령
press (media)	*sinmun* (sheen-muun)	신문
price	*kap* (kahp)	값
(half price)	*pan kap* (pahn-kahp)	반값
priest	*shinbu* (sheen-buu)	신부
principle	*wonchik* (wun-cheek)	원칙
printing	*inswae* (een-sway)	인쇄
private	*satchogin* (saht-chuh-geen)	사적인
private room	*pyol shil* (p'yohl sheel)	별실
profession	*chigop* (chee-gup)	직업
professional	*chigobui* (chee-gub-wee)	직업의
professor	*kyosu* (k'yoh-suh)	교수
profit	*iik* (eeek)	이익
program	*puroguraem* (puu-roh-guu-ram)	프로그램
project	*kyehoek* (kay-hoak)	계획
province	*to/do* (doh)	도
puncture	*pongku* (pung-kuu)	펑크
push	*miroyo* (me-ru-yoh)	밀어요

[Q]

qualifications	*chagyok* (choh-gyuhk)	자격
quality	*tuksong* (duuk-sohng)	특성
quantity	*yang* (yahng)	양
quarantine	*kyongni* (k'yuhng-nee)	격리
question	*chilmun* (cheel-muun)	질문
quickly	*ppalli* (bahl-lee)	빨리
quiet	*chojonghan* (choh-johng-hahn)	조용한
quit (give up)	*kumanduda* (kuh-mahn-duu-dah)	그만두다

[R]

rabbi	*rappinim* (rap-bee-neem)	랍비님
race (breed)	*injong* (en-johng)	인종
racism	*injong chabyol* (en-johng chah-byuhl)	인종 차별
radio	*radio* (rah-dee-oh)	라디오
railroad	*choldo* (chohl-doh)	철도
railway station	*kicha yok* (kee-chah yuhk)	기차역
rain	*pi* (pee)	비
raincoat	*reinkotu* (rain-koh-tuu)	레인코트
rainy day	*pionun nal* (pee-oh-nuun nahl)	비오는 날
rainy season	*changma chol* (chahng-mah chohl)	장마철
rank	*chiwi* (chee-we)	지위
rash (skin)	*pahchin* (pahl-cheen)	발진
raw (uncooked)	*nalgosui* (nahl-guh-swee)	날것의
raw fish	*nal-saeng-suhn* (nahl-saeng-sang)	날생선
razor	*myondokal* (m'yohn-doh-kahl)	면도칼
razor blades	*myondokal* (m'yohn-doh-kahl)	면도칼
receipt	*yongsujung* (yahng-suu-jahng)	영수증
reference	*chamjo* (chahm-joh)	참조
refrigerator	*naengjanggo* (nayng-jahng-go)	냉장고
refund	*hwanbul* (hwahn-buhl)	환불
region	*chibang* (chee-bahng)	지방
registered mail	*tunggi upyon* (tuhng-ghee uu-p'yun)	등기 우편
relative (kin)	*chinchok* (cheen-choak)	친척
religion	*chonggyo* (chohng-g'yoh)	종교
remote control	*rimo kon* (ree-moh kohn)	리모콘

rent	*pilda* (peel-dah)	빌다
repair shop	*chong biso* (chohng bee-soh)	정비소
reservation	*yeyak* (yay-yahk)	예약
reserved seat	*chijong sok* (chee-johng suk)	지정석
responsibility	*chaegim* (chay-geem)	책임
rest	*hushik* (huu-sheek)	휴식
restaurant	*shiktang* (sheek-tahng)	식당
restroom	*hwajang shil* (hwa-jahng sheel)	화장실
resume	*iryokso* (eer-yuhk-suh)	이력서
rice (cooked)	*pap* (pahp)	밥
rice wine	*chong jong* (chohng johng)	정종
rich (wealthy)	*tonmanhun* (dohn-mahn-huhn)	돈많은
ring (for finger)	*panji* (pahn-jee)	반지
river	*kang* (kahng)	강
road	*toro* (doh-roh)	도로
road map	*torojido* (doh-roh-jee-doh)	도로지도
romance	*aejong* (aa-johng)	애정
room	*pang* (pahng)	방
room service	*rum sobisu* (rume sah-bee-suu)	룸 서비스
rush hour	*roshiawo* (rah-she-ah-wah)	러시아워
Russia	*Roshia* (Ruh-she-ah)	러시아

[S]

safe (for valuables)	*kumgo* (kuum-go)	금고
salary	*ponggup* (pohng-guhp)	봉급
sample	*kyonbon* (kyuhn-bohn)	견본
sandwich	*sanduwichi* (sand-we-chee)	샌드위치
sanitary napkins	*saeng nidae* (sang nee-day)	생리대
satellite dish	*wisongjopshi antena* (we-suung-juhp-she antenna)	위성접시 안테나

sauna	*sauna* (sow-nah)	사우나
schedule	*siganpyo* (she-gahn-p'yoh)	시간표
scholar	*hakcha* (hahk-chah)	학자
school	*hakkkyo* (hahk-k'yoh)	학교
science	*kwahak* (kwah-hahk)	과학
scissors	*kawi* (kah-we)	가위
scrambled eggs	*pokkun dalgyal* (poke-kuhn dahl-g'yahl)	볶은 달걀
scroll	*chokja* (choak-jah)	족자
seafood	*hoemul* (hway-muhl)	해물
seashore	*hae-byon* (hie-b'yohn)	해변
seasons	*kyejol* (keh-juhl)	계절
seatbelt	*anjon beltu* (ahn-jun bel-tuu)	안전 벨트
seaweed (toasted)	*kim* (keem)	김
second-class seat	*i-dung sok* (ee-duhng suhk)	이등석
secretary	*piso* (bee-suh)	비서
self-service	*selpu sobisu* (selp-uu sah-bee-suu)	셀프서비스
service (help)	*sobisu* (sah-bee-suu)	서비스
service charge	*sobisu ryo* (sah-be-suu rio)	서비스료
sex	*song* (suhng)	성
sex (the act)	*seksu* (sek-suu)	섹스
sexual harassment	*song hirong* (suhng he-rohng)	성회롱
sexy	*sekshihan* (sek-she-hahn)	섹시한
ship	*pae* (pay)	배
shirt	*shochu* (shah-chuh)	셔츠
shoeshine	*kududakki* (kuu-duu-dahk-kee)	구두닦이
shop (place)	*kage* (kah-gay)	가게
shopping	*shop'ing* (shop-eeng)	쇼핑
shopping arcade	*shop'ing akeidu* (shop-eeng ah-kay-ee-doh)	쇼핑 아케이드

121

short (length)	*tchalbun* (chahl-buhn)	짧은
shower	*shawo* (shah-wuh)	샤워
shrine	*sadang* (sah-dahng)	사당
shuttle bus	*shotul bosu* (shuttle bah-suu)	셔틀버스
sightseeing	*kugyong* (kuu-g'yohng)	구경
signature	*somyong* (suhm-yuhng)	서명
silk	*pidan* (pee-dahn)	비단
singer	*kasu* (kah-suu)	가수
single (person)	*shinggul* (sheeng-guhl)	싱글
single room	*shinggul rum* (sheeng-guhl ruum)	싱글룸
size (fit)	*saiju* (sigh-juu)	사이즈
ski	*suki* (suu-kee)	스키
ski resort	*suki rijotu* (suuk-kee ree-joh-tuu)	스키 리조트
sleep	*cham* (chahm)	잠
smoke (tobacco)	*tambae* (dahm-bay)	담배
smoking area	*hubyon kuyok* (huh-byun kuu-yuhk)	흡연구역
snow	*nun* (nun)	눈
snowstorm	*nunbora* (nun-boh-rah)	눈보라
soldier	*gunin* (guun-een)	군인
South Korea	*Nam Han* (Nahm Hahn)	남한
souvenir	*kinyompum* (kee-n'yohm-pume)	기념품
souvenir shop	*kinyompum kage* (kee-n'yohm-pume kah-geh)	기념품 가게
speaker	*yonsa* (yuhn-sah)	연사
guest speaker	*chochong yonsa* (choh-chuung yuhn-sah)	초청 연사
speed limit	*chehan sokto* (chay-hahn soke-toh)	제한 속도
spicy (hot)	*maeun* (may-uun)	매운
sports	*undong* (uun-dohng)	운동

sprain	*ppida* (beep-dah)	삐다
sprained ankle	*palmogul ppiossumnida* (pahl-moh-guhl pee-ah-ssume-nee-dah)	팔목을 삐었습니다
stadium	*undongjang* (uun-dohng-jahng)	운동장
staff (personnel)	*chigwon* (chee-gwuhn)	직원
steak	*suteiku* (su-tay-kuu)	스테이크
stomachache	*poktong* (poke-tohng)	복통
stop (halt)	*momchuda* (muum-chuu-dah)	멈추다
stop (place)	*chungji* (chuung-jee)	정지
street	*toro* (doh-roh)	도로
stroke (illness)	*choltto* (chohl-toh)	졸도
student	*haksaeng* (hahk-sang)	학생
suburb	*kyooe* (k'yoh-whay)	교외
sugar	*solfang* (sohl-fahng)	설탕
suggestion	*amsi* (ahm-shee)	암시
suit (law)	*sosong* (so-song)	소송
sunglasses	*songullasu* (sun-guh-lah-suu)	선글라스
sweater	*suweto* (swea-tah)	스웨터
sweetheart	*yonin* (yuhn-een)	연인
swimming pool	*suyong jang* (suu-yohng jahng)	수영장
swim suit	*suyong bok* (suu-yohng boak)	수영복
symbol	*sangjing* (sahng-jeeng)	상징
synagogue	*yutaegyo hodang* (yuu-tay-g'yoh hoh-dahng)	유태교회당
system	*chegye* (chay-gay)	체계

[T]

table	*takcha* (tahk-chah)	탁자
table tennis	*tak kut* (tahk kute)	탁구

tailor	*yangbokjom* (yahg-boak-jome)	양복점
Taiwan	*Taeman* (Tay-mahn)	대만
tax	*segum* (say-gume)	세금
taxi	*taekshi* (tack-she)	택시
taxi stand	*taekshi sunggangjang* (tack-she suhng-gahng-jahng)	택시 승강장
teacher	*sonsaengnim* (suun-sang-neem)	선생님
television	*terebijon* (tay-ray-bee-joan)	테레비전
temperature (weather)	*kion* (kee-own)	기온
temple (Buddhist)	*chol* (chohl)	절
terminal (domestic)	*kungnae chongsa* (kuhng-nay chung-sah)	국내 청사
test	*sihom* (she-huhm)	시험
theater (movie)	*kukchang* (kuhk-chahng)	극장
theory	*iron* (ee-roan)	이론
thermometer	*cheongye* (chohn-gay)	체온계
ticket counter	*pyo panungot* (p'yoh pah-nuhn-got)	표 파는 곳
ticket vending machine	*pyo chapangi* (p'yoh chah-pahn-ghee)	표 자판기
tissue	*tishyu* (tee-shuu)	티슈
toast (bread)	*tostu* (tos-tuu)	토스트
toast (drinking)	*konbae haeyo* (kom-bay hay-yoh)	건배해요
tongue	*hyo* (h'yoh)	혀
toothpick	*issushigae* (ees-shu-she-gay)	이쑤시개
tour (travel)	*tuo* (tu-ah)	투어
tourist	*yohaenggaek* (yoh-hang-gake)	여행객
traffic	*kyotong* (k'yoh-tohng)	교통
tranquilizers	*chinjongje* (cheen-johng-jay)	진정제

trees	*namu* (nah-muu)	나무
trousers	*paji* (pah-jee)	바지
truck	*turok* (tuu-ruk)	트럭
trust (believe)	*shinyong* (sheen-yohng)	신용
truth	*chilli* (cheel-lee)	진리
truth (fact)	*sasil* (sah-sheel)	사실
tunnel	*tonol* (tuh-nuhl)	터널
typhoon	*taepung* (tay-puung)	태풍

[U]

umbrella	*usan* (uu-sahn)	우산
umpire	*shimpan* (sheem-pahn)	심판
uncle	*ajossi* (ah-juh-she)	아저씨
underground passage	*chihado* (jee-hah-doh)	지하도
underground shopping center	*chiha sangga* (jee-hah sahng-gah)	지하 상가
unfair	*pulgongpyonghan* (puhl-gohng-p'yung-hahn)	불공평한
unification	*tongil* (tohng-eel)	통일
uniform	*chebok* (chay-boak)	제복
university	*taehakkkyo* (day-hahk-k'yoh)	대학교
untrue	*kojishin* (kuh-jee-sheen)	거짓인
USA	*Miguk* (Me-guuk)	미국

[V]

vacancy (room)	*pin bang* (peen bahng)	빈 방
vacant	*pin* (peen)	빈
vacant house	*pin jip* (peen jeep)	빈 집
vacation	*hyuga* (hyuu-gah)	휴가
vaccination	*chongdu* (chohng-duu)	종두
valid	*yuhyohan* (yuu-h'yoh-hahn)	유효한
valley	*koltchagi* (kohl-chah-ghee)	골짜기

valuables	*kwijungpum* (kwee-juung-pume)	귀중품
value	*kachi* (kah-chee)	가치
vegetarian	*chaeshikchuuija* (chay-sheek-chuu-we-jah)	채식주의자
vegetable(s)	*yachae* (yah-chay)	야채
vendor (seller)	*haengsangin* (hang-sahng-een)	행상인
veteran (expert)	*noryon-ga* (noh-r'yuhn-gah)	노련가
veteran (soldier)	*nobyong* (noh-byung)	노병
view	*kyongchi* (k'yohng-chee)	경치
village	*maul* (mah-uhl)	마을
virgin	*sungyorhan* (suung-yuhr-han)	순결한
visa	*pija* (bee-jah)	비자
visitor (guest)	*sonnim* (soan-neem)	손님
vitamins	*bitamin* (bee-tah-meen)	비타민
volcano	*hwasan* (hwah-sahn)	화산
volleyball	*paegu* (pay-guu)	배구
voltage	*chon-ap* (chone-ahp)	전압
volume	*yang* (yahng)	양
vomit	*tohada* (toh-hah-dah)	토하다
vote (n)	*tupyo* (tup-yoh)	투표

[W]

wage	*imgum* (eem-guhm)	임금
wait (for)	*kidarida* (kee-dah-ree-dah)	기다리다
waiter	*weito* (way-tah)	웨이터
waitress	*weituresu* (way-tuu-reh-suu)	웨이트레스
walk (stroll)	*sanpo* (sahn-poh)	산보
wallet	*chigap* (chee-gahp)	지갑
war	*chonjaeng* (chohng-jang)	전쟁

watch (timepiece)	*shigye* (she-gay)	시계
waterfall	*pok-po* (poak-poh)	폭포
watermelon	*subak* (suu-bahk)	수박
waves (water)	*pado* (pah-doh)	파도
weapon	*mugi* (muu-ghee)	무기
weather	*nalssi* (nahl-she)	날씨
weather forecast	*ilgi yebo* (eel-ghee yay-boh)	일기예보
wedding	*kyorhon* (kyuhr-hone)	결혼
wedding anniversary	*kyorhon kinyomil* (kyuhr-hone keen yuh-meel)	결혼기념일
weigh	*muge-rul talda* (muu-gay-ruhl tahl-dah)	무게를 달다
weight	*muge* (muu-gay)	무게
west (direction)	*sotchok* (suht-chock)	서쪽
Western (cowboy movie)	*seobu yonghwa* (say-buu yohng-hwah)	서부 영화
whale	*korae* (koh-ray)	고래
wheat	*mil* (meel)	밀
whisky	*wisuki* (wis-kee)	위스키
wholesale	*tomae* (toh-may)	도매
wholesaler	*tomae sangin* (toh-may sahng-een)	도매 상인
widow	*mimangin* (me-mahng-een)	미망인
widower	*horabi* (hoh-rah-bee)	홀아비
win (gain)	*awtta* (awt-dah)	얻다
wind	*param* (pah-rahm)	바람
window	*changmun* (chanhng-muun)	창문
windy	*param punun* (pah-rahm puu-nuhn)	바람 부는
wine (grape)	*podoju* (boh-doh-juu)	포도주
wireless	*musonui* (muu-suhn-we)	무선의

world	*segye* (seh-gay)	세계
wrap (package)	*pojanghada* (poh-jahng-hah-dah)	포장하다
wreck (destroy)	*pagoehada* (pah-gway-hah-dah)	파괴하다
wrestling	*resulling* (ray-suhl-leeng)	레슬링
wristwatch	*sonmokshigye* (sohn-moke-she-gay)	손목시계
write	*ssuda* (suh-dah)	쓰다
wrong (error)	*chalmot* (chal-mote)	잘못

[XYZ]

X-ray	*eks-rei* (x-ray)	엑스레이
yacht	*yotu* (yah-tuu)	요트
yard	*madang* (mah-dahng)	마당
year (n)	*hae* (hay)	해
young	*cholmun* (chuhl-muhn)	젊은
zero	*yong* (yuhng)	영
zipper	*chipo* (jee-pah)	지퍼
zone (region)	*chidae* (chee-day)	지대
zoo	*tongmurwon* (dohng-muhr-wuhn)	동물원

BAramb Peyoung chireep

BELL 쓰 myun

cheat if Chreep

Jugo

Qui